The Art of Shaping
LIVES

James Allen (1864–1912) retired from the business world to pursue a lifestyle of writing and contemplation. His books are classics in the fields of inspiration and spirituality. Although *As a Man Thinketh* is his most popular work, he authored several other books that deal with the power of thought, including *The Path of Prosperity*, *Eight Pillars of Prosperity* and *James Allen's Book of Meditations for Every Day in the Year.*

The Art of Shaping
LIVES

Mastering Your Own **Destiny**

JAMES ALLEN

RUPA

Published by
Rupa Publications India Pvt. Ltd 2024
7/16, Ansari Road, Daryaganj
New Delhi 110002

Sales Centres:
Bengaluru Chennai
Hyderabad Jaipur Kathmandu
Kolkata Mumbai Prayagraj

P-ISBN: 978-93-5702-877-6
E-ISBN: 978-93-5702-675-8

First impression 2024

10 9 8 7 6 5 4 3 2 1

Printed in India

CONTENTS

1

DEEDS, CHARACTER, AND DESTINY

There is, and always has been, a widespread belief in Fate, or Destiny, that is, in an eternal and inscrutable Power which apportions definite ends to both individuals and nations. This belief has arisen from long observation of the facts of life.

Men are conscious that there are certain occurrences which they cannot control, and are powerless to avert. Birth and death, for instance, are inevitable, and many of the incidents of life appear equally inevitable.

Men strain every nerve for the attainment of certain ends, and gradually they become conscious of a Power which seems to be not of themselves, which frustrates their puny efforts, and laughs, as it were, at their fruitless striving and struggle.

As men advance in life, they learn to submit, more or less, to this overruling Power which they do not understand, perceiving only its effects in themselves and the world around them, and they call it by various names, such as God, Providence, Fate, Destiny, etc.

Men of contemplation, such as poets and philosophers, step aside, as it were, to watch the movements of this mysterious Power as it seems to elevate its favorites on the one hand, and strike down its victims on the other, without reference to merit or demerit.

The greatest poets, especially the dramatic poets, represent this Power in their works, as they have observed it in Nature. The Greek and Roman dramatists usually depict their heroes as having foreknowledge of their fate, and taking means to escape it; but by so doing they blindly involve themselves in a series of consequences which bring about the doom which they are trying to avert. Shakespeare's characters, on the other hand, are represented, as in Nature, with no foreknowledge (except in the form of presentiment) of their particular destiny. Thus, according to the poets, whether the man knows his fate or not, he cannot avert it, and every conscious or unconscious act of his is a step towards it.

Omar Khayyam's Moving Finger is a vivid expression of this idea of Fate:

"The Moving Finger writes, and having writ,
Moves on: nor all thy Piety nor Wit
Shall lure it back to cancel half a line,
Nor all thy Tears wash out a Word of it."

Thus, men in all nations and times have experienced in their lives the action of this invincible Power or Law, and in our nation today this experience has been crystallized in the terse proverb, "Man proposes, God disposes."

But, contradictory as it may appear, there is an equally widespread belief in man's responsibility as a free agent.

All moral teaching is an affirmation of man's freedom to choose his course and mold his destiny: and man's patient and untiring efforts in achieving his ends are declarations of consciousness of freedom and power.

This dual experience of fate on the one hand, and freedom on the other, has given rise to the interminable controversy between the believers in Fatalism and the upholders of free will——a controversy which was recently revived under the term "Determinism versus Freewill."

Between apparently conflicting extremes there is always a

"middle way" of balance, justice, or compensation which, while it includes both extremes, cannot be said to be either one or the other, and which brings both into harmony; and this middle way is the point of contact between two extremes.

Truth cannot be a partisan, but, by its nature, is the Reconciler of extremes; and so, in the matter which we are considering, there is a "golden mean" which brings Fate and Free will into close relationship, wherein, indeed, it is seen that these two indisputable facts in human life, for such they are, are but two aspects of one central law, one unifying and all-embracing principle, namely, the law of causation in its moral aspect.

Moral causation necessitates both Fate and Free will, both individual responsibility and individual predestination, for the law of causes must also be the law of effects, and cause and effect must always be equal; the train of causation, both in matter and mind, must be eternally balanced, therefore eternally just, eternally perfect. Thus every effect may be said to be a thing preordained, but the predetermining power is a cause, and not the fiat of an arbitrary will.

Man finds himself involved in the train of causation. His life is made up of causes and effects. It is both a sowing and a reaping. Each act of his is a cause which must be balanced by its effects. He chooses the cause (this is Free will), he cannot choose, alter, or avert the effect (this is Fate); thus Free will stands for the power to initiate causes, and destiny is involvement in effects.

It is therefore true that man is predestined to certain ends, but he himself has (though he knows it not) issued the mandate; that good or evil thing from which there is no escape, he has, by his own deeds, brought about.

It may here be urged that man is not responsible for his

deeds, that these are the effects of his character, and that he is not responsible for the character, good or bad, which was given him at his birth. If character was "given him" at birth, this would be true, and there would then be no moral law, and no need for moral teaching; but characters are not given ready made, they are evolved; they are, indeed, effects, the products of the moral law itself, that is—the products of deeds. Character result of an accumulation of deeds which have been piled up, so to speak, by the individual during his life.

Is There a Perfect Man?

Man is the doer of his own deeds; as such he is the maker of his own character; and as the doer of his deeds and the maker of his character, he is the molder and shaper of his destiny. He has the power to modify and alter his deeds, and every time he acts he modifies his character, and with the modification of his character for good or evil, he is predetermining for himself new destinies—destinies disastrous or beneficent in accordance with the nature of his deeds. Character is destiny itself; as a fixed combination of deeds, it bears within itself the results of those deeds. These results lie hidden as moral seeds in the dark recesses of the character, awaiting their season of germination, growth, and fruitage.

Those things which befall a man are the reflections of himself; that destiny which pursued him, which he was powerless to escape by effort, or avert by prayer, was the relentless ghoul of his own wrong deeds demanding and enforcing restitution; those blessings and curses which come to him unbidden are the reverberating echoes of the sounds which he himself sent forth.

It is this knowledge of the Perfect Law working through and above all things; of the Perfect Justice operating in and adjusting all human affairs, that enables the good man to love his enemies, and to rise above all hatred, resentment, and complaining; for he knows that only his own can come to him, and that, though he be surrounded by persecutors, his enemies are but the blind instruments of a faultless retribution; and so he blames them not, but calmly receives his accounts, and patiently pays his moral debts.

But this is not all; he does not merely pay his debts; he takes care not to contract any further debts. He watches himself and makes his deeds faultless. While paying off evil accounts, he is laying up good accounts. By putting an end to his own sin, he is bringing evil and suffering to an end.

And now let us consider how the Law operates in particular instances in the outworking of destiny through deeds and character. First, we will look at this present life, for the present is the synthesis of the entire past; the net result of all that a man has ever thought and done is contained within him. It is noticeable that sometimes the good man fails and the unscrupulous man prospers—a fact which seems to put all moral maxims as to the good results of righteousness out of account—and because of this, many people deny the operation of any just law in human life, and even declare that it is chiefly the unjust that prosper.

Nevertheless, the moral law exists, and is not altered or subverted by shallow conclusions. It should be remembered that man is a changing, evolving being. The good man was not always good; the bad man was not always bad. Even in this life, there was a time, in a large number of instances, when the man who is now just, was unjust; when he who is now kind, was cruel; when he who is now pure, was impure.

Conversely, there was a time in this life, in a number of instances, when he who is now unjust, was just; when he who is now cruel, was kind; when he who is now impure, was pure.

Thus, the good man who is overtaken with calamity today is reaping the result of his former evil sowing; later he will reap the happy result of his present good sowing; while the bad man is now reaping the result of his former good sowing; later he will reap the result of his present sowing of bad.

Characteristics are fixed habits of mind, the results of deeds. An act repeated a large number of times becomes unconscious, or automatic—that is, it then seems to repeat itself without any effort on the part of the doer, so that it seems to him almost impossible not to do it, and then it has become a mental characteristic.

Here is a poor man out of work. He is honest, and is not a shirker. He wants work, and cannot get it. He tries hard, and continues to fail. Where is the justice in his lot? There was a time in this man's condition when he had plenty of work. He felt burdened with it; he shirked it, and longed for ease. He thought how delightful it would be to have nothing to do.

He did not appreciate the blessedness of his lot. His desire for ease is now gratified, but the fruit for which he longed, and which he thought would taste so sweet, has turned to ashes in his mouth. The condition which he aimed for, namely, to have nothing to do, he has reached, and there he is compelled to remain till his lesson is thoroughly learned.

And he is surely learning that habitual ease is degrading, that to have nothing to do is a condition of wretchedness, and that work is a noble and blessed thing. His former desires and deeds have brought him where he is; and now his present desire for work, his ceaseless searching and asking for it, will just as surely bring about its own beneficent result. No longer desiring idleness, his present condition will, as an effect, the cause of which is no longer propagated, soon pass away, and he will obtain employment; and if his whole mind is now set on work, and he desires it above all else, then when it comes he will be overwhelmed with it; it will flow in to him from all sides, and he will prosper in his industry.

Then, if he does not understand the law of cause and effect in human life, he will wonder why work comes to him apparently unsought, while others who seek it strenuously fail to obtain it. Nothing comes unbidden; where the shadow is, there also is the substance. That which comes to the individual is the product of his own deeds.

As cheerful industry leads to greater industry and increasing prosperity, and labor shirked or undertaken discontentedly leads to a lesser degree of labor and decreasing prosperity, so with all the varied conditions of life as we see them—they are the destinies wrought by the thoughts and deeds of each particular individual. So also with the vast variety of characters—they are the ripening and ripened growth of the sowing of deeds.

As the individual reaps what he sows, so the nation, being a community of individuals, reaps also what it sows. Nations become great when their leaders are just men; they fall and fade when their just men pass away. Those who are in power set an example, good or bad, for the entire nation.

Great will be the peace and prosperity of a nation when there shall arise within it a line of statesmen who, having first established themselves in a lofty integrity of character, shall direct the energies of the nation toward the culture of virtue and development of character, knowing that only through personal industry, integrity, and nobility can national prosperity proceed.

Still, above all, is the Great Law, calmly and with infallible justice meting out to mortals their fleeting destinies, tear-stained or smiling, the fabric of their hands. Life is a great school for the development of character, and all, through strife and struggle, vice and virtue, success and failure, are slowly but surely learning the lessons of wisdom.

2

ENERGY AND POWER

How wonderful is the universal energy! Never-tiring, inexhaustible, and apparently eternal in its operation, it moves in atom and in star, informing the fleeting shapes of tune with its restless, glowing, pulsating power.

Man is a portion of this creative energy, and in him it manifests, through a combination of mental faculties, as affection, passion, intelligence, morality, reason, understanding, and wisdom. He is not merely a blind conductor of energy, but he consciously uses, controls, and directs it. Slowly, but with certainty, is he gaining control of the forces without, and is making them do obedient service. And just as surely will he gain control of the forces within—the subtle energies of thought—and direct them into channels of harmony and happiness.

Man's true place in the Cosmos is that of a king, not a slave, a commander under the law of Good and not a helpless tool in the reign of Evil. His own body and mind are the dual dominion over which he is to reign, a Lord of Truth, the master of himself, the wise user and controller of his store of pure, eternal, creative energy. Let him walk the earth unashamed, strong, valiant, tender, and kind; no longer prostrate in self-abasement, but walking erect in the dignity of perfect manhood; not groveling in selfishness and remorse, nor crying for pardon and mercy, but standing firm and free in the sublime majesty of a sinless life.

Long has man regarded himself as vile, weak, and unworthy,

and has been content to remain so. But in the new era which has just now burst upon the world, he is to make a glorious discovery that he is pure, powerful, and noble when he rises up and wills. The rising up is not against any outward enemy; not against neighbor, nor governments, nor laws, nor spirits, nor principalities, but against the ignorance, folly, and misery which beset him in the dominion of his own mind. For it is only by ignorance and folly that man is slavish; by knowledge and wisdom his kingdom is restored.

Let them who will, preach man's weakness and helplessness, but I will teach his strength and power. I write for men, not for babes; for those who are eager to learn, and earnest to achieve; for those who will put away (for the world's good) a petty personal indulgence, a selfish desire, a mean thought, and live on as though it were not, without craving and regret. The Truth is not for the frivolous and the thoughtless. The Life Triumphant is not for triflers and loiterers.

Man is a master. If he were not, he could not act contrary to law. Thus his so-called weakness is an indication of strength; his sin is the inversion of his capacity for holiness. For what is his weakness and sin but misdirected energy, misapplied power? In this sense, the wrongdoer is strong, not weak; but he is ignorant, and exerts his strength in wrong directions instead of right, against the law of things instead of with it.

Suffering is the recoil of misdirected strength, The bad man becomes good by reversing his conduct. If you are weeping over your sins, cease to commit those sins and establish yourself in their opposing virtues. It is thus that weakness is converted into strength, helplessness into power, and suffering into bliss. By turning his energies from the old channels of vice, and directing them into the new channels of virtue, the sinner becomes a saint.

Use and Misuse of Energy

While the universal energy may be unlimited, in particular forms its sum is strictly limited. A man is possessed of a given amount of energy, and he can use it or misuse it, can conserve and concentrate it, or dissipate and disperse it. Power is concentrated energy; wisdom is that energy adapted to beneficent ends. He is the man of influence and power who directs all his energies towards one great purpose, and patiently works and waits for its fulfillment, sacrificing his desires in other and more pleasant directions. He is the man of folly and weakness who, thinking chiefly of pleasure, gratifies the desire of the hour, or follows the whim and impulse of the moment, and so drifts thoughtlessly into peevishness and poverty of mind.

The energy used in one direction is not available for use in other directions; this is a universal law both in mind and matter. Emerson calls it "the law of compensation." Gain in a given direction necessitates loss in its opposite direction. The force placed in one scale is deducted from the other scale. Nature is always endeavoring to strike a balance. The energy which is dissipated in idleness is not given to work. The pleasure-seeker cannot also be a Truth-seeker.

The force wasted in a fit of bad temper is drawn from the man's store of virtue, particularly the virtue of patience. Spiritually, this law of compensation is the law of sacrifice. Selfish pleasure must be sacrificed if purity is to be gained; hatred must be yielded up if love is to be acquired; vice must be renounced if virtue is to be embraced.

Earnest men soon discover that if they are to accomplish anything that is successful, strong, and enduring, in worldly, intellectual, or spiritual channels, they must curb their desires, and sacrifice much that seems sweet; yea, even much that seems important.

Hobbies, bodily and mental indulgences, enticing companionships, alluring pleasures, and all work that does not tend to some central purpose in his life must be sacrificed by the man of strong resolve. He opens his eyes to the fact that time and energy are strictly limited, and so he economizes the one and concentrates the other.

Foolish men waste their energies in swinish ease and gluttonous indulgence, in frivolous pleasures and empty talk, in hateful thoughts and irritable outbursts of passion, in vain controversy and meddlesome interference. They then complain that many are more "fortunately equipped than they are for a useful, successful, or great life, and they envy their honored neighbor who has sacrificed self to duty, and has devoted all his energies to the faithful performance of the business of his life.

"He who is just, speaks the truth, and does what is his own business, him the world will hold dear." Let a man attend to his own business, concentrating all his energies upon the perfect accomplishment of the task of his life, not stepping aside to condemn or interfere with the duties of others, and he will find life simple, strong, and happy.

The Truth of Life

The universe is girt with goodness and strength, and it protects the strong and the good. Evil and weakness are self-destructive. Dissipation is annihilation. All nature loves strength. I see no inherent cruelty in "the survival of the fittest." It is a spiritual as well as a natural law. The stronger qualities of the beast are the fittest to evolve a higher type. The nobler moral qualities in man are his emancipators, and it is well that they should dominate and ultimately crush out the ignoble tendencies.

Most certain it is that he who gives dominion to the lower, courts destruction, and does not survive, either in the struggle of life without or the battle of Truth within. The life given to the lower is lost to the higher; yea, it is finally lost also to the lower, and so all is lost, for evil is ultimately nothingness. But the life given to the higher is preserved, and is not lost to anything, for, while it sacrifices much that the world holds precious, it does not sacrifice anything that is precious in reality.

The untrue and worthless must perish, and he who consecrates himself to the good and the true is content that they should perish, and so at last he stands where sacrifice ends, and all is gain—such a one survives in the struggle of life without, and he conquers in the battle of Truth within.

First, then, be strong. Strength is the firm basis on which is built the temple of the Triumphant Life.

Without a central motive and fixed resolve, your life will be a poor, weak, drifting, unstable thing. Let the act of the moment be governed by the deep abiding purpose of the heart. You will act differently at different times, but the act will not be wrong if the heart is right. You may fall and go astray at times, especially under great stress, but you will quickly regain yourself, and you will grow wiser and stronger, thereby, so long as you guide yourself by the moral compass within, and do not throw it away to gratify indulgence and give yourself up to uncertain drifting.

Follow your conscience. Be true to your convictions. Do at the moment what you regard as right, and put away all procrastination, vacillation, and fear. If you are convinced that in the performance of your duty under certain circumstances the severest measures are necessary, carry out those measures, and let there be no uncertainty about it. Err on the side of strength rather than weakness. The measures you adopt may not be the best, but if they are the best you know, then your plain duty is to carry them out. By so doing you will discover the better way, if you are anxious for progress, and are willing to learn. Deliberate beforehand, but in the tune of action do not hesitate.

Avoid anger and stubbornness, lust and greed. The angry man is the weak man. The stubborn man, who refuses to learn or mend his ways, is the foolish man. He grows old in folly, and grey hairs do not bring him reverence or honor. The sensualist has energy for pleasure only, and reserves none for manliness and self-respect. The greedy man is blind to the nobility of human nature and the glory of a true life; he spends his energies in perpetuating the miseries of hell, instead of enjoying the happiness of heaven.

Your strength is with you, and you can spend it in burrowing downward or in climbing upward. You can dissipate it in selfishness or conserve it in goodness. The same energy will enable you to become a beast or a god. The course along which you direct it will determine its effect. Do not think the thought, "My mind is weak," but convert weakness into strength, and energy into power by redirecting your mental forces. Turn your thoughts into noble channels. Put away vain longings and foolish regrets; abolish complaint and self-condolence, and have no dalliance with evil. Lift your face upward. Rise up in your divine strength, and spurn from your mind and life all meanness and weakness. Do not live the false life of a whining slave, but live the true life of a conquering master.

3

THE INNER WORLD OF THOUGHTS

Man is the maker of happiness and misery. Further, he is the creator and perpetuator of his own happiness and misery. These things are not externally imposed; they are internal conditions. Their cause is neither deity, nor devil, nor circumstance, but Thought. They are the effects of deeds, and deeds are the visible side of thoughts. Fixed attitudes of mind determine courses of conduct, and from courses of conduct come those reactions called happiness and unhappiness. This being so, it follows that, to alter the reactive condition, one must alter the active thought. To exchange misery for happiness it is necessary to reverse the fixed attitude of mind and habitual course of conduct which is the cause of misery, and the reversed effect will appear in the mind and life. A man has no power to be happy while thinking and acting selfishly; he cannot be unhappy while thinking and acting unselfishly. Wheresoever the cause is, there the effect will appear. Man cannot abrogate effects, but he can alter causes. He can purify his nature; he can remould his character. There is great power in self-conquest; there is great joy in transforming oneself.

Each man is circumscribed by his own thoughts, but he can gradually extend their circle; he can enlarge and elevate his mental sphere. He can leave the low, and reach up to the high; he can refrain from harbouring thoughts that are dark and hateful, and can cherish thoughts that are bright and beautiful; and as he does his, he will pass into a higher sphere of power and beauty, will become conscious of a more complete and perfect world.

For men live in spheres low or high according to the nature of their thoughts. Their world is as dark and narrow as they conceive it to be, as expansive and glorious as their comprehensive capacity. Everything around them is tinged with the colour of their thoughts.

Consider the man whose mind is suspicious, covetous, envious. How small and mean and drear everything appears to him. Having no grandeur in himself, he sees no grandeur anywhere; being ignoble himself, he is incapable of seeing nobility in any being. Even his God is a covetous being that can be bribed, and he judges all men and women to be just as petty and selfish as he himself is, so that he sees in the most exalted acts of unselfishness only motives that are mean and base.

Consider again the man whose mind is unsuspecting, generous, magnanimous. How wondrous and beautiful is his world. He is conscious of some kind of nobility in all creatures and beings. He sees men as true, and to him they are true. In his presence the meanest forget their nature, and for the moment become like himself, getting a glimpse, albeit confused, in that temporary upliftments of a higher order of things, of an immeasurably nobler and happier life.

That small-minded, and this large-hearted, man live in two different worlds, though they be neighbours. Their consciousness embraces totally different principles. Their actions are each the reverse of the other. Their moral insight is contrary. They each look out upon a different order of things. Their mental spheres are separate, and, like two detached circles, they never mingle. The one is in hell, the other in heaven as truly as they will ever be, and death will not place a greater gulf between them than already exists. To the one, the world is a den of thieves; to the other, it is the dwelling-place of Gods. The one keeps a revolver handy, and is always on his guard against being robbed or cheated (unconscious of the fact that he is all the time robbing and cheating himself), the other keeps ready a banquet for the best. He throws open his doors to talent, beauty, genius, goodness. His friends are of the aristocracy of character. They have become a part of himself. They are in his sphere of thought, his world of consciousness. From his heart pours forth nobility, and it returns to him tenfold in the multitude of those who love him and do him honour.

Each Man His Own

The natural grades in human society—what are they but spheres of thought, and modes of conduct manifesting those spheres? The proletariat may rail against these divisions, but he will not alter or affect them. There is no artificial remedy for equalising states of thought having no natural affinity, and separated by the fundamental principles of life. The lawless and the law-abiding are eternally apart, nor is it hatred nor pride that separates them, but states of intelligence and modes of conduct which in the moral principles of things stand mutually unrelated. The rude and ill-mannered are shut out from the circle of the gentle and refined by the impassable wall of their own mentality which, though they may remove by patient self-improvement, they can never scale by a vulgar intrusion. The kingdom of heaven is not taken by violence, but he who conforms to its principles receives the password. The ruffian moves in a society of ruffians; the saint is one of an elect brethren whose communion is divine music. All men are mirrors reflecting according to their own surface. All men, looking at the world of men and things, are looking into a mirror which gives back their own reflection.

Each man moves in the limited or expansive circle of his own thoughts, and all outside that circle is non-existent to him. He only knows that which he has become. The narrower the boundary, the more convinced is the man that there is no further limit, no other circle. The lesser cannot contain the greater, and he has no means of apprehending the larger minds; such knowledge comes only by growth. The man who moves in a widely extended circle of thought knows all the lesser circles from which he has emerged, for in the larger experience all lesser experiences are contained and preserved; and when his circle impinges upon the sphere of perfect manhood, when he is fitting himself for company and communion with them of blameless conduct and profound understanding, then his wisdom will have become sufficient to convince him that there are wider circles still beyond of which he is as yet but dimly conscious, or is entirely ignorant.

Men, like schoolboys, find themselves in standards or classes to which their ignorance or knowledge entitles them. The curriculum of the sixth standard is a mystery to the boy in the first; it is outside and beyond the circle of his comprehension; but he reaches it by persistent effort and patient growth in learning. By mastering and outgrowing all the standards between, he comes at last to the sixth, and makes its learning his own; and beyond still is the sphere of the teacher. So in life, men whose deeds are dark and selfish, full of passion and personal desire, cannot comprehend those whose deeds are bright and unselfish, whose minds are calm, deep, and pure, but they can reach this higher standard, this enlarged consciousness, by effort in right doing, by growth in thought and moral comprehension. And above and beyond all lower and higher standards stand the Teachers of mankind, the Cosmic Masters, the Saviours of the world whom the adherents of the various religions worship.

There are grades in teachers as in pupils, and some there are who have not yet reached the rank and position of Master, yet, by the sterling morality of their character, are guides and teachers; but to occupy a pulpit or rostrum does not make a man a teacher. A man is constituted a teacher by virtue of that moral greatness which calls forth the respect and reverence of mankind.

Each man is as low or high, as little or great, as base or noble as his thoughts; no more, no less. Each moves within the sphere of his own thoughts, and that sphere is his world. In that world in which he forms his habits of thought, he finds his company. He dwells in the region which harmonises with his particular growth. But he need not perforce remain in the lower worlds. He can lift his thoughts and ascend. He can pass above and beyond into higher realms, into happier habitations. When he chooses and wills he can break the carapace of selfish thought, and breathe the purer airs of a more expansive life.

4

THE OUTER WORLD OF THINGS

The world of things is the other half of the world of thoughts. The inner informs the outer. The greater embraces the lesser. Matter is the counterpart of mind. Events are streams of thought. Circumstances are combinations of thought, and the outer conditions and actions of others in which each man is involved are intimately related to his own mental needs and development. Man is a part of his surroundings. He is not separate from his fellows, but is bound closely to them by the peculiar intimacy and interaction of deeds, and by those fundamental laws of thought which are the roots of human society.

One cannot alter external things to suit his passing whims and wishes, but he can set aside his whims and wishes; he can so alter his attitude of mind towards externals that they will assume a different aspect. He cannot mould the actions of others towards him, but he can rightly fashion his actions towards them. He cannot break down the wall of circumstance by which he is surrounded, but he can wisely adapt himself to it, or find the way out into enlarged circumstances by extending his mental horizon. Things follow thoughts. Alter your thoughts, and things will receive a new adjustment. To reflect truly the mirror must be true. A warped glass gives back an exaggerated image. A disturbed mind gives a distorted reflection of the world. Subdue the mind, organise and tranquillise it, and a more beautiful image of the universe, a more prefect perception of the world-order will be the result.

The Cause and Effect Force in Universe

Man has all power within the world of his own mind, to purify and perfect it; but his power in the outer world of other minds is subject and limited. This is made plain when we reflect that each finds himself in a world of men and things, a unit amongst myriads of similar units. These units do not act independently and despotically, but responsively and sympathetically. My fellow-men are involved in my actions, and they will deal with them. If what I do be a menace to them, they will adopt protective measures against me. As the human body expels its morbid atoms, so the body politic instinctively expurgates its recalcitrant members. Your wrong acts are so many wounds inflicted on this body politic, and the healing of its wounds will be your pain and sorrow. This ethical cause and effect is not different from that physical cause and effect with which the simplest is acquainted. It is but an extension of the same law; its application to the larger body of humanity. No act is aloof. Your most secret deed is invisibly reported, its good being protected in joy, its evil destroyed in pain. There is a great ethical truth in the old fable of "the Book of Life," in which every thought and deed is recorded and judged. It is because of this—that your deed belongs, not alone to yourself, but to humanity and the universe—that you are powerless to avert external effects, but are all-powerful to modify and correct internal causes; and it is also because of this that the perfecting of one's own deeds is man's highest duty and most sublime accomplishment.

The obverse of this truth—that you are powerless to obviate external things and deeds—is, that external things and deeds are powerless to injure you. The cause of your bondage as of your deliverance is within. The injury that comes to you through others is the rebound of your own deed, the reflex of your own mental attitude. They are the instruments, you are the cause. Destiny is ripened deeds. The fruit of life, both bitter and sweet, is received by each man in just measure. The righteous man is free. None can injure him; none can destroy him; none can rob him of his peace. His attitude towards men, born of understanding, disarms their power to wound him. Any injury which they may try to inflict, rebounds upon themselves to their own hurt, leaving him unharmed and untouched. The good that goes from him is his perennial fount of happiness, his eternal source of strength. Its root is serenity, its flower is joy.

The harm which a man sees in the action of another towards him—say, for instance, an act of slander—is not in the act itself, but in his attitude of mind towards it; the injury and unhappiness are created by himself, and subsist in his lack of understanding concerning the nature and power of deeds. He thinks the act can permanently injure or ruin his character, whereas it is utterly void of any such power; the reality being that the deed can only injure or ruin the doer of it. Thinking himself injured, the man becomes agitated and unhappy, and takes great pains to counteract the supposed harm to himself, and these very pains give the slander an appearance of truth, and aid rather than hinder it. All his agitation and unrest is created by his reception of the deed, and not actually by the deed itself. The righteous man has proved this by the fact that the same act has ceased to arouse in him any disturbance. He understands, and therefore ignores, it. It belongs to a sphere which he has ceased to inhabit, to a region of consciousness with which he has no longer any affinity. He does not receive the act into himself, the thought of injury to himself being absent. He lives above the mental darkness in which such acts thrive, and they can no more injure or disturb him than a boy can injure or divert the sun by throwing stones at it. It was to emphasise this that Buddha, to the end of his days, never ceased to tell his disciples that so long as the thought "I have been injured," or "I have been cheated," or "I have been insulted," could arise in a man's mind, he had not comprehended the Truth.

And as with the conduct of others, so is it with external things—with surroundings and circumstances—in themselves they are neither good nor bad, it is the mental attitude and state of heart that makes them so. A man imagines he could do great things if he were not hampered by circumstances—by want of money, want of time, want of influence, and want of freedom from family ties. In reality the man is not hindered by these things at all. He, in his mind, ascribes to them a power which they do not possess, and he submits not to them, but to his opinion about them, that is, to a weak element in his nature. The real "want" that hampers him is the want of the right attitude of mind. When he regards his circumstances as spurs to his resources, when he sees that his so-called "drawbacks" are the very steps up which he is to mount successfully to his achievement, then his necessity gives birth to invention, and the "hindrances" are transformed into aids. The man is the all-important factor. If his mind be wholesome and rightly tuned, he will not whine and whimper over his circumstances, but will rise up, and outgrow them. He who complains of his circumstances has not yet become a man, and Necessity will continue to prick and lash him till he rises into manhood's strength, and then she will submit to him. Circumstance is a severe taskmaster to the weak, an obedient servant to the strong.

It is not external things, but our thoughts about them, that bind us or set us free. We forge our own chains, build our own dungeons, take ourselves prisoners; or we loose our bonds, build our own palaces, or roam in freedom through all scenes and events. If I think that my surroundings are powerful to bind me, that thought will keep me bound. If I think that, in my thought and life, I can rise above my surroundings, that thought will liberate me. One should ask of his thoughts, "Are they leading to bondage or deliverance?" and he should abandon thoughts that bind, and adopt thoughts that set free.

If we fear our fellow-men, fear opinion, poverty, the withdrawal of friends and influence, then we are bound indeed, and cannot know the inward happiness of the enlightened, the freedom of the just; but if in our thoughts we are pure and free, if we see in life's reactions and reverses nothing to cause us trouble or fear, but everything to aid us in our progress, nothing remains that can prevent us from accomplishing the aims of our life, for then we are free indeed.

5

CAUSE AND EFFECT IN HUMAN CONDUCT

It is an axiom with the scientists that every effect is related to a cause. Apply this to the realm of human conduct, and the principle of Justice is revealed.

Every scientist knows (and now all men believe) that perfect harmony prevails throughout every portion of the physical universe, from the speck of dust to the greatest sun. Everywhere there is exquisite adjustment. In the sidereal universe, with its millions of suns rolling majestically through space and carrying with them their respective systems of revolving planets, its vast nebula, its seas of meteors, and its vast army of comets traveling through illimitable space with inconceivable velocity, perfect order prevails; and again, in the natural world, with its multitudinous aspects of life, and its infinite variety of forms, there are the clearly defined limits of specific laws, through the operation of which all confusion is avoided, and unity and harmony eternally obtain.

If this universal harmony could be arbitrarily broken, even in one small particular, the universe would cease to be; there could be no cosmos, but only universal chaos. Nor can it be possible in such a universe of law that there should exist any personal power which is above, outside, and superior to, such law in the sense that it can defy it, or set it aside; for whatsoever beings exist, whether they be men or gods, they exist by virtue of such law; and the highest, best, and wisest among all beings would manifest his greater wisdom by his more complete obedience to that law which is wiser than wisdom, and than which nothing more perfect could be devised.

All things, whether visible or invisible, are subservient to, and fall within the scope of, this infinite and eternal law of causation. As all things seen obey it, so all things unseen—the thoughts and deeds of men, whether secret or open—cannot escape it.

"Do right, it recompenseth; do one wrong, The equal retribution must be made."

What Goes Around, Comes Around

Perfect justice upholds the universe; perfect justice regulates human life and conduct. All the varying conditions of life, as they obtain in the world today, are the result of this law reacting on human conduct. Man can (and does) choose what causes he shall set in operation, but he cannot change the nature of effects; he can decide what thoughts he shall think, and what deeds he shall do, but he has no power over the results of those thoughts and deeds; these are regulated by the overruling law.

Man has all power to act, but his power ends with the act committed. The result of the act cannot be altered, annulled, or escaped; it is irrevocable. Evil thoughts and deeds produce conditions of suffering; good thoughts and deeds determine conditions of blessedness. Thus man's power is limited to, and his blessedness or misery is determined by his own conduct. To know this truth, renders life simple, plain, and unmistakable; all the crooked paths are straightened out, the heights of wisdom are revealed, and the open door to salvation from evil and suffering is perceived and entered.

Life may be likened to a sum in arithmetic. It is bewilderingly difficult and complex to the pupil who has not yet grasped the key to its correct solution, but once this is perceived and laid hold of, it becomes as astonishingly simple as it was formerly profoundly perplexing. Some idea of this relative simplicity and complexity of life may be grasped by fully recognizing and realizing the fact that, while there are scores, and perhaps hundreds, of ways in which a sum may be done wrong, there is only one way by which it can be done right, and that when that right way is found the pupil knows it to be the right; his perplexity vanishes, and he knows that he has mastered the problem.

It is true that the pupil, while doing his sum incorrectly, may (and frequently does) think he has done it correctly, but he is not sure; his perplexity is still there, and if he is an earnest and apt pupil, he will recognize his own error when it is pointed out by the teacher. So in life, men may think they are living rightly while they are continuing, through ignorance, to live wrongly; but the presence of doubt, perplexity, and unhappiness are sure indications that the right way has not yet been found.

There are foolish and careless pupils who would like to pass a sum as correct before they have acquired a true knowledge of figures, but the eye and skill of the teacher quickly detect and expose the fallacy. So in life there can be no falsifying of results; the eye of the Great Law reveals and exposes. Twice five will make ten to all eternity, and no amount of ignorance, stupidity, or delusion can bring the result up to eleven.

If one looks superficially at a piece of cloth, he sees it as a piece of cloth, but if he goes further and inquires into its manufacture, and examines it closely and attentively, he sees that it is composed of a combination of individual threads, and that, while all the threads are interdependent, each thread pursues its own way throughout, never becoming confused with its sister thread. It is this entire absence of confusion between the particular threads which constitutes the finished work a piece of cloth; any inharmonious commingling of the thread would result in a bundle of waste or a useless rag.

Life is like a piece of cloth, and the threads of which it is composed are individual lives. The threads, while being interdependent, are not confounded one with the other. Each follows its own course. Each individual suffers and enjoys the consequences of his own deeds, and not of the deeds of another. The course of each is simple and definite; the whole forming a complicated, yet harmonious, combination of sequences. There are action and reaction, deed and consequence, cause and effect, and the counterbalancing reaction, consequence, and effect is always in exact ratio with the initiatory impulse.

A durable and satisfactory piece of cloth cannot be made from shoddy material, and the threads of selfish thoughts and bad deeds will not produce a useful and beautiful life—a life that will wear well, and bear close inspection. Each man makes or mars his own life; it is not made or marred by his neighbor, or by anything external to himself. Each thought he thinks, each deed he does, is another thread—shoddy or genuine—woven into the garment of his life; and as he makes the garment so must he wear it. He is not responsible for his neighbor's deeds; he is not the custodian of his neighbor's actions; he is responsible only for his own deeds; he is the custodian of his own actions.

The "problem of evil" subsists in a man's own evil deeds, and it is solved when those deeds are purified. Says Rousseau:

"Man, seek no longer the origin of evil; thou thyself art its origin."

Effect can never be divorced from cause; it can never be of a different nature from cause. Emerson says:

"Justice is not postponed; a perfect equity adjusts the balance in all parts of life."

And there is a profound sense in which cause and effect are simultaneous, and form one perfect whole. Thus, upon the instant that a man thinks, say, a cruel thought, or does a cruel deed, that same instant he has injured his own mind; he is not the same man he was the previous instant; he is a little viler and a little more unhappy; and a number of such successive thoughts and deeds would produce a cruel and wretched man. The same thing applies to the contrary—the thinking of a kind thought, or doing a kind deed—an immediate nobility and happiness attend it; the man is better than he was before, and a number of such deeds would produce a great and blissful soul.

Thus individual human conduct determines, by the faultless law of cause and effect, individual merit or demerit, individual greatness or meanness, individual happiness or wretchedness. What a man thinks, that he does; what he does, that he is. If he is perplexed, unhappy, restless, or wretched, let him look to himself, for there and nowhere else is the source of all his trouble.

6

RIGHT PRINCIPLES

It is wise to know what comes first, and what to do first. To begin anything in the middle or at the end is to make a muddle of it. The athlete who began by breaking the tape would not receive the prize. He must begin by facing the starter and toeing the mark, and even then a good start is important if he is to win. The pupil does not begin with algebra and literature, but with counting and ABC. So in life—the businessmen who begin at the bottom achieve the more enduring success; and the religious men who reach the highest heights of spiritual knowledge and wisdom are they who have stooped to serve a patient apprenticeship to the humbler tasks, and have not scorned the common experiences of humanity, or overlooked the lessons to be learned from them.

The first things in a sound life—and therefore, in a truly happy and successful life—are right principles. Without right principles to begin with, there will be wrong practices to follow with, and a bungled and wretched life to end with. All the infinite variety of calculations which tabulate the commerce and science of the world, come out of the ten figures; all the hundreds of thousands of books which constitute the literature of the world, and perpetuate its thought and genius, are built up from the twenty-six letters. The greatest astronomer cannot ignore the ten simple figures. The profoundest man of genius cannot dispense with the twenty-six simple characters. The fundamentals in all things are few and simple: yet without them there is no knowledge and no achievement. The fundamentals—the basic principles—in life, or true living, are also few and simple, and to learn them thoroughly, and study how to apply them to all the details of life, is to avoid confusion, and to secure a substantial foundation for the orderly building up of an invincible character and a permanent success; and to succeed in comprehending those principles in their innumerable ramifications in the labyrinth of conduct, is to become a Master of Life.

Five Fingers Make a Fist

The first principles in life are principles of conduct. To name them is easy. As mere words they are on all men's lips, but as fixed sources of action, admitting of no compromise, few have learned them. In this short talk I will deal with five only of these principles. These five are among the simplest of the root principles of life, but they are those that come nearest to the everyday life, for they touch the artisan the businessman, the householder, the citizen at every point. Not one of them can be dispensed with but at severe cost, and he who perfects himself in their application will rise superior to many of the troubles and failures of life, and will come into these springs and currents of thought which flow harmoniously towards the regions of enduring success. The first of these principles is:

Duty—A much-hackneyed word, I know, but it contains a rare jewel for him who will seek it by assiduous application. The principle of duty means strict adherence to one's own business, and just as strict non-interference in the business of others. The man who is continually instructing others, gratis, how to manage their affairs, is the one who most mismanages his own. Duty also means undivided attention to the matter in hand, intelligent concentration of the mind on the work to be done; it includes all that is meant by thoroughness, exactness, and efficiency. The details of duties differ with individuals, and each man should know his own duty better then he knows his neighbour's, and better than his neighbour knows his; but although the working details differ, the principle is always the same. Who has mastered the demands of duty?

Honesty is the next principle. It means not cheating or overcharging another. It involves the absence of all trickery, lying, and deception by word, look, or gesture. It includes sincerity, the saying what you mean, and the meaning what you say. It scorns cringing policy and shining compliment. It builds up good reputations, and good reputations build up good businesses, and bright joy accompanies well-earned success. Who has scaled the heights of Honesty?

Economy is the third principle. The conservation of one's financial resources is merely the vestibule leading towards the more spacious chambers of true economy. It means, as well, the husbanding of one's physical vitality and mental resources. It demands the conservation of energy by the avoidance of enervating self-indulgences and sensual habits. It holds for its follower strength, endurance, vigilance, and capacity to achieve. It bestows great power on him who learns it well. Who has realized the supreme strength of Economy?

Liberality follows economy. It is not opposed to it. Only the man of economy can afford to be generous. The spendthrift, whether in money, vitality, or mental energy, wasted so much on his own miserable pleasures as to have none left to bestow upon others. The giving of money is the smallest part of liberality. There is a giving of thoughts, and deeds, and sympathy, the bestowing of goodwill, the being generous towards calumniators and opponents. It is a principle that begets a noble, far-reaching influence. It brings loving friends and staunch comrades, and is the foe of loneliness and despair. Who has measured the breadth of Liberality?

Self-Control is the last of these five principles, yet the most important. Its neglect is the cause of vast misery, innumerable failures, and tens of thousands of financial, physical, and mental wrecks. Show me the businessman who loses his temper with a customer over some trivial matter, and I will show you a man who, by that condition of mind, is doomed to failure. If all men practised even the initial stages of self-control, anger, with its consuming and destroying fire, would be unknown. The lessons of patience, purity, gentleness, kindness, and steadfastness, which are contained in the principle of self-control, are slowly learned by men, yet until they are truly learned a man's character and success are uncertain and insecure. Where is the man who has perfected himself in Self-Control? Where he may be, he is a master indeed.

The five principles are five practices, five avenues to achievement, and five sources of knowledge. It is an old saying and a good rule that "Practice makes perfect," and he who would make his own the wisdom which is inherent in those principles, must not merely have them on his lips, they must be established in his heart. To know them and receive what they alone can bring, he must do them, and give them out in his actions.

7

MIND-BUILDING AND LIFE-BUILDING

Everything, both in nature and the works of man, is produced by a process of building. The rock is built up of atoms; the plant, the animal, and man are built up of cells; a house is built of bricks, and a book is built of letters. A world is composed of a large number of forms, and a city of a large number of houses. The arts, sciences, and institutions of a nation are built up by the efforts of individuals. The history of a nation is the building of its deeds.

The process of building necessitates the alternate process of breaking down. Old forms that have served their purpose are broken up, and the material of which they are composed enters into new combinations. There is reciprocal integration and disintegration. In all compounded bodies, old cells are ceaselessly being broken up, and new cells are formed to take their place.

The works of man also require to be continually renewed until they have become old and useless, when they are torn down in order that some better purpose may be served. These two processes of breaking down and building up in Nature are called death and life; in the artificial works of man they are called destruction and restoration.

This dual process, which obtains universally in things visible, also obtains universally in things invisible. As a body is built of cells, and a house of bricks, so a man's mind is built of thoughts. The various characters of men are none other than compounds of thoughts of varying combinations. Herein we see the deep truth of the saying, "As a man thinketh in his heart, so is he." Individual characteristics are fixed processes of thought; that is, they are fixed in the sense that they have become such an integral part of the character that they can be only altered or removed by a protracted effort of the will, and by much self-discipline. Character is built in the same way as a tree or a house is built—namely, by the ceaseless addition of new material, and that material is thought. By the aid of millions of bricks a city is built; by the aid of millions of thoughts a mind, a character, is built.

Every man is a mind builder, whether he recognizes it or not. Every man must perforce think, and every thought is another brick laid down in the edifice of mind. Such "brick laying" is done loosely and carelessly by a vast number of people, the result being unstable and tottering characters that are ready to go down under the first little gust of trouble or temptation.

Some, also, put into the building of their minds large numbers of impure thoughts; these are so many rotten bricks that crumble away as fast as they are put in, leaving always an unfinished and unsightly building, and one which can afford no comfort and no shelter for its possessor.

Debilitating thoughts about one's health, enervating thoughts concerning unlawful pleasures, weakening thoughts of failure, and sickly thoughts of self-pity and self-praise are useless bricks with which no substantial mind temple can be raised.

Pure thoughts, wisely chosen and well placed, are so many durable bricks which will never crumble away, and from which a finished and beautiful building, and one which affords comfort and shelter for its possessor, can be rapidly erected.

Bracing thoughts of strength, of confidence, of duty;

inspiring thoughts of a large, free, unfettered, and unselfish life, are useful bricks with which a substantial mind temple can be raised; and the building of such a temple necessitates that old and useless habits of thought be broken down and destroyed.

"Build thee more stately mansions, O my soul! As the swift seasons roll."

Each man is the builder of himself. If he is the occupant of a jerry-built hovel of a mind that lets in the rains of many troubles, and through which blow the keen winds of oft-recurring disappointments, let him get to work to build a more noble mansion which will afford him better protection against those mental elements. Trying to weakly shift the responsibility for his jerry-building on to the devil, or his forefathers, or anything or anybody but himself, will neither add to his comfort, nor help him to build a better habitation.

When he wakes up to a sense of his responsibility, and an approximate estimate of his power, then he will commence to build like a true workman, and will produce a symmetrical and finished character that will endure, and be cherished by posterity, and which, while affording a never failing protection for himself, will continue to give shelter to many a struggling one when he has passed away.

The whole visible universe is framed on a few mathematical principles. All the wonderful works of man in the material world have been brought about by the rigid observance of a few underlying principles; and all that there is to the making of a successful, happy, and beautiful life, is the knowledge and application of a few simple, root principles.

If a man is to erect a building that is to resist the fiercest storms, he must build it on a simple, mathematical principle, or law, such as the square or the circle; if he ignores this, his edifice will topple down even before it is finished.

Likewise, if a man is to build up a successful, strong, and exemplary life—a life that will stoutly resist the fiercest storms of adversity and temptation—it must be framed on a few simple, undeviating moral principles.

Four of these principles are Justice, Rectitude, Sincerity, and Kindness. These four ethical truths are to the making of a life what the four lines of a square are to the building of a house. If a man ignores them and thinks to obtain success and happiness and peace by injustice, trickery, and selfishness, he is in the position of a builder who imagines he can build a strong and durable habitation while ignoring the relative arrangement of mathematical lines, and he will, in the end, obtain only disappointment and failure.

He may, for a time, make money, which will delude him into believing that injustice and dishonesty pay well; but in reality his life is so weak and unstable that it is ready at any moment to fall; and when a critical period comes, as come it must, his affairs, his reputation, and his riches crumble to ruins, and he is buried in his own desolation.

It is totally impossible for a man to achieve a truly successful and happy life who ignores the four moral principles enumerated, whilst the man who scrupulously observes them in all his dealings can no more fail of success and blessedness than the earth can fail of the light and warmth of the sun so long as it keeps to its lawful orbit; for he is working in harmony with the fundamental laws of the universe; he is building his life on a basis which cannot be altered or overthrown, and, therefore, all that he does will be so strong and durable, and all the parts of his life will be so coherent, harmonious, and firmly knit that it cannot possibly be brought to ruin.

The Foundation of Happiness

In all the universal forms which are built up by the Great Invisible and unerring Power, it will be found that the observance of mathematical law is carried out with unfailing exactitude down to the most minute detail. The microscope reveals the fact that the infinitely small is as perfect as the infinitely great.

A snowflake is as perfect as a star. Likewise, in the erection of a building by man, the strictest attention must be paid to every detail.

A foundation must first be laid, and, although it is to be buried and hidden, it must receive the greatest care, and be made stronger than any other part of the building; then stone upon stone, brick upon brick is carefully laid with the aid of the plumb line, until at last the building stands complete in its durability, strength, and beauty.

Even so it is with the life of a man. He who would have a life secure and blessed, a life freed from the miseries and failures to which so many fall victims, must carry the practice of the moral principles into every detail of his life, into every momentary duty and trivial transaction. In every little thing he need be thorough and honest, neglecting nothing.

To neglect or misapply any little detail—be he commercial man, agriculturist, professional man, or artisan—is the same as neglecting a stone or a brick in a building, and it will be a source of weakness and trouble.

The majority of those who fail and come to grief do so through neglecting the apparently insignificant details.

It is a common error to suppose that little things can be passed by, and that the greater things are more important, and should receive all attention; but a cursory glance at the universe, as well as a little serious reflection on life, will teach the lesson that nothing great can exist which is not made up of small details, and in the composition of which every detail is perfect.

He who adopts the four ethical principles as the law and base of his life, who raises the edifice of character upon them, who in his thoughts and words and actions does not wander from them, whose every duty and every passing transaction is performed in strict accordance with their exactions, such a man, laying down the hidden foundation of integrity of heart securely and strongly, cannot fail to raise up a structure which shall bring him honor; and he is building a temple in which he can repose in peace and blessedness—even the strong and beautiful Temple of his life.

8

VISIONS AND IDEALS

The dreamers are the saviours of the world. As the visible world is sustained by the invisible, so men, through all their trials and sins and sordid vocations, are nourished by the beautiful visions of their solitary dreamers. Humanity cannot forget its dreamers; it cannot let their ideals fade and die; it lives in them; it knows them as they realities which it shall one day see and know.

Composer, sculptor, painter, poet, prophet, sage, these are the makers of the after-world, the architects of heaven. The world is beautiful because they have lived; without them, labouring humanity would perish.

He who cherishes a beautiful vision, a lofty ideal in his heart, will one day realize it. Columbus cherished a vision of another world, and he discovered it; Copernicus fostered the vision of a multiplicity of worlds and a wider universe, and he revealed it; Buddha beheld the vision of a spiritual world of stainless beauty and perfect peace, and he entered into it.

Cherish your visions; cherish your ideals; cherish the music that stirs in your heart, the beauty that forms in your mind, the loveliness that drapes your purest thoughts, for out of them will grow all delightful conditions, all, heavenly environment; of these, if you but remain true to them, your world will at last be built.

To desire is to obtain; to aspire is to, achieve. Shall man's basest desires receive the fullest measure of gratification, and his purest aspirations starve for lack of sustenance? Such is not the Law: such a condition of things can never obtain: "ask and receive."

Dream lofty dreams, and as you dream, so shall you become. Your Vision is the promise of what you shall one day be; your Ideal is the prophecy of what you shall at last unveil.

The greatest achievement was at first and for a time a dream. The oak sleeps in the acorn; the bird waits in the egg; and in the highest vision of the soul a waking angel stirs. Dreams are the seedlings of realities.

Becoming Your Vision

Your circumstances may be uncongenial, but they shall not long remain so if you but perceive an Ideal and strive to reach it. You cannot travel within and stand still without. Here is a youth hard pressed by poverty and labour; confined long hours in an unhealthy workshop; unschooled, and lacking all the arts of refinement. But he dreams of better things; he thinks of intelligence, of refinement, of grace and beauty. He conceives of, mentally builds up, an ideal condition of life; the vision of a wider liberty and a larger scope takes possession of him; unrest urges him to action, and he utilizes all his spare time and means, small though they are, to the development of his latent powers and resources. Very soon so altered has his mind become that the workshop can no longer hold him. It has become so out of harmony with his mentality that it falls out of his life as a garment is cast aside, and, with the growth of opportunities, which fit the scope of his expanding powers, he passes out of it forever. Years later we see this youth as a full-grown man. We find him a master of certain forces of the mind, which he wields with worldwide influence and almost unequalled power. In his hands he holds the cords of gigantic responsibilities; he speaks, and lo, lives are changed; men and women hang upon his words and remould their characters, and, sunlike, he becomes the fixed and luminous centre round which innumerable destinies revolve. He has realized the Vision of his youth. He has become one with his Ideal.

And you, too, youthful reader, will realize the Vision (not the idle wish) of your heart, be it base or beautiful, or a mixture of both, for you will always gravitate toward that which you, secretly, most love. Into your hands will be placed the exact results of your own thoughts; you will receive that which you earn; no more, no less. Whatever your present environment may be, you will fall, remain, or rise with your thoughts, your Vision, your Ideal. You will become as small as your controlling desire; as great as your dominant aspiration: in the beautiful words of Stanton Kirkham Davis, "You may be keeping accounts, and presently you shall walk out of the door that for so long has seemed to you the barrier of your ideals, and shall find yourself before an audience—the pen still behind your ear, the ink stains on your fingers and then and there shall pour out the torrent of your inspiration. You may be driving sheep, and you shall wander to the city-bucolic and open-mouthed; shall wander under the intrepid guidance of the spirit into the studio of the master, and after a time he shall say, 'I have nothing more to teach you.' And now you have become the master, who did so recently dream of great things while driving sheep. You shall lay down the saw and the plane to take upon yourself the regeneration of the world."

The thoughtless, the ignorant, and the indolent, seeing only the apparent effects of things and not the things themselves, talk of luck, of fortune, and chance. Seeing a man grow rich, they say, "How lucky he is!" Observing another become intellectual, they exclaim, "How highly favoured he is!" And noting the saintly character and wide influence of another, they remark, "How chance aids him at every turn!" They do not see the trials and failures and struggles which these men have voluntarily encountered in order to gain their experience; have no knowledge of the sacrifices they have made, of the undaunted efforts they have put forth, of the faith they have exercised, that they might overcome the apparently insurmountable, and realize the Vision of their heart. They do not know the darkness and the heartaches; they only see the light and joy, and call it "luck". They do not see the long and arduous journey, but only behold the pleasant goal, and call it "good fortune," do not understand the process, but only perceive the result, and call it chance.

In all human affairs there are efforts, and there are results, and the strength of the effort is the measure of the result. Chance is not. Gifts, powers, material, intellectual, and spiritual possessions are the fruits of effort; they are thoughts completed, objects accomplished, visions realized.

The Vision that you glorify in your mind, the Ideal that you enthrone in your heart—this you will build your life by, this you will become.

9

THE POWER OF PURPOSE

Dispersion is weakness; concentration is power. Destruction is a scattering, preservation a uniting, process. Things are useful and thoughts are powerful in the measure that their parts are strongly and intelligently concentrated. Purpose is highly concentrated thought.

All the mental energies are directed to the attainment of an object, and obstacles which intervene between the thinker and the object are, one after another, broken down and overcome. Purpose is the keystone in the temple of achievement. It binds and holds together in a complete whole that which would otherwise lie scattered and useless.

Empty whims, ephemeral fancies, vague desires, and half-hearted resolutions have no place in purpose. In the sustained determination to accomplish there is an invincible power which swallows up all inferior considerations, and marches direct to victory.

All successful men are men of purpose. They hold fast to an idea, a project, a plan, and will not let it go; they cherish it, brood upon it, tend and develop it; and when assailed by difficulties, they refuse to be beguiled into surrender; indeed, the intensity of the purpose increases with the growing magnitude of the obstacles encountered.

The men who have molded the destinies of humanity have been men mighty of purpose. Like the Roman laying his road, they have followed along a well defined path, and have refused to swerve aside even when torture and death confronted them. The Great Leaders of the race are the mental road makers, and mankind follows in the intellectual and spiritual paths which they have carved out and beaten.

The Pen Is Mightier than the Sword

Great is the power of purpose. To know how great, let a man study it in the lives of those whose influence has shaped the ends of nations and directed the destinies of the world. In an Alexander, a Caesar, or a Napoleon, we see the power of purpose when it is directed in worldly and personal channels; in a Confucius, a Buddha, or a Christ, we perceive its vaster power when its course is along heavenly and impersonal paths.

Purpose goes with intelligence. There are lesser and greater purposes according with degrees of intelligence. A great mind will always be great of purpose. A weak intelligence will be without purpose. A drifting mind argues a measure of undevelopment.

What can resist an unshakable purpose? What can stand against it or turn it aside? Inert matter yields to a living force, and circumstance succumbs to the power of purpose. Truly, the man of unlawful purpose will, in achieving his ends, destroy himself, but the man of good and lawful purpose cannot fail. It only needs that he daily renew the fire and energy of his fixed resolve, to consummate his object.

The weak man, who grieves because he is misunderstood, will not greatly achieve; the vain man, who steps aside from his resolve in order to please others and gain their approbation, will not highly achieve; the double minded man, who thinks to compromise his purpose, will fail.

The man of fixed purpose who, whether misunderstandings and foul accusations, or flatteries and fair promises, rain upon him, does not yield a fraction of his resolve, is the man of excellence and achievement; of success, greatness, power.

Hindrances stimulate the man of purpose; difficulties nerve him to renewed exertion; mistakes, losses, pains, do not subdue him; and failures are steps in the ladder of success, for he is ever conscious of the certainty of final achievement.

All things at last yield to the silent, irresistible, all conquering energy of purpose.

"Out of the night that covers me,
Black as the pit from pole to pole,
I thank whatever gods may be
For my unconquerable soul.
In the fell clutch of circumstance
I have not whined nor cried aloud;
Under the bludgeoning of chance
My head is bloody but unbowed.
It matters not how strait the gate,
How charged with punishment the scroll;
I am the master of my fate,
I am the captain of my soul."

10

TRAINING OF THE WILL

Without strength of mind, nothing worthy of accomplishment can be done, and the cultivation of that steadfastness and stability of character which is commonly called "willpower" is one of the foremost duties of man, for its possession is essentially necessary both to his temporal and eternal well being. Fixedness of purpose is at the root of all successful efforts, whether in things worldly or spiritual, and without it man cannot be otherwise than wretched, and dependent upon others for that support which should be found within himself.

The mystery which has been thrown around the subject of cultivation of the will by those who advertise to sell "occult advice" on the matter for so many dollars, should be avoided and dispelled, for nothing could be further removed from secrecy and mystery than the practical methods by which alone strength of will can be developed.

The true path of will cultivation is only to be found in the common everyday life of the individual, and so obvious and simple is it that the majority, looking for something complicated and mysterious, pass it by unnoticed.

The Science of Will Cultivation

A little logical thought will soon convince a man that he cannot be both weak and strong at the same time, that he cannot develop a stronger will while remaining a slave to weak indulgences, and that, therefore, the direct and only way to that greater strength is to assail and conquer his weaknesses. All the means for the cultivation of the will are already at hand in the mind and life of the individual; they reside in the weak side of his character, by attacking and vanquishing which the necessary strength of will be developed. He who has succeeded in grasping this simple, preliminary truth, will perceive that the whole science of will cultivation is embodied in the following seven rules:

1. Break off bad habits.
2. Form good habits.
3. Give scrupulous attention to the duty of the present moment.
4. Do vigorously, and at once, whatever has to be done.
5. Live by rule.
6. Control the tongue.
7. Control the mind.

Anyone who earnestly meditates upon, and diligently practices, the above rules, will not fail to develop that purity of purpose and power of will which will enable him to successfully cope with every difficulty, and pass triumphantly through every emergency.

It will be seen that the first step is the breaking away from bad habits. This is no easy task. It demands the putting forth of great efforts, or a succession of efforts, and it is by such efforts that the will can alone be invigorated and fortified. If one refuses to take the first step, he cannot increase in willpower, for by submitting to a bad habit, because of the immediate pleasure which it affords, one forfeits the right to rule over himself, and is so far a weak slave. He who thus avoids self-discipline, and looks about for some "occult secrets" for gaining willpower at the expenditure of little or no effort on his part, is deluding himself, and is weakening the willpower which he already possesses.

The increased strength of will which is gained by success in overcoming bad habits enables one to initiate good habits; for, while the conquering of a bad habit requires merely strength of purpose, the forming of a new one necessitates the intelligent direction of purpose. To do this, a man must be mentally active and energetic, and must keep a constant watch upon himself. As a man succeeds in perfecting himself in the second rule, it will not be very difficult for him to observe the third, that of giving scrupulous attention to the duty of the present moment.

Thoroughness is a step in the development of the will which cannot be passed over. Slipshod work is an indication of weakness. Perfection should be aimed at, even in the smallest task. By not dividing the mind, but giving the whole attention to each separate task as it presents itself, singleness of purpose and intense concentration of mind are gradually gained—two mental powers which give weight and worth of character, and bring repose and joy to their possessor.

The fourth rule—that of doing vigorously, and at once, whatever has to be done—is equally important. Idleness and a strong will cannot go together, and procrastination is a total barrier to the acquisition of purposeful action. Nothing should be "put off" until another time, not even for a few minutes. That which ought to be done now should be done now. This seems a little thing, but it is of far reaching importance. It leads to strength, success, and peace.

The man who is to manifest a cultivated will must also live by certain fixed rules. He must not blindly gratify his passions and impulses, but must school them to obedience. He should live according to principle, and not according to passion.

He should decide what he will eat and drink and wear, and what he will not eat and drink and wear; how many meals per day he will have, and at what times he will have them; at what time he will go to bed, and at what time get up. He should make rules for the right government of his conduct in every department of his life, and should religiously adhere to them. To live loosely and indiscriminately, eating and drinking and sensually indulging at the beck and call of appetite and inclination, is to be a mere animal, and not a man with will and reason.

The beast in man must be scourged and disciplined and brought into subjection, and this can only be done by training the mind and life on certain fixed rules of right conduct. The saint attains to holiness by not violating his vows, and the man who lives according to good and fixed rules, is strong to accomplish his purpose.

The sixth rule, that of controlling the tongue, must be practiced until one has perfect command of his speech, so that he utters nothing in peevishness, anger, irritability, or with evil intent. The man of strong will does not allow his tongue to run thoughtlessly and without check.

All these six rules, if faithfully practiced, will lead up to the seventh, which is the most important of them all—namely, rightly controlling the mind. Self-control is the most essential thing in life, yet least understood; but he who patiently practices the rules herein laid down, bringing them into requisition in all his ways and undertakings, will learn, by his own experience and efforts, how to control and train his mind, and to earn thereby the supreme crown of manhood—the crown of a perfectly poised will.

11

TEMPTATION

Aspiration can carry a man into heaven, but to remain there, he must learn to conform his entire mind to the heavenly conditions. To this end temptation works.

Temptation is the reversion, in thought, from purity to passion. It is going back from aspiration to desire. It threatens aspiration until the point is reached where desire is quenched in the waters of pure knowledge and calm thought.

In the early stages of aspiration, temptation is subtle and powerful, and is regarded as an enemy; but it is only an enemy in the sense that the one tempted is his own enemy. In the sense that it is the revealer of weakness and impurity, it is a friend, a necessary factor in spiritual training. It is, indeed, an accompaniment of the effort to overcome evil and apprehend good. To be successfully conquered, the evil in a man must come to the surface and present itself, and it is in temptation that the evil hidden in the heart stands revealed and exposed.

That which temptation appeals to and arouses is unconquered desire, and temptation will again and again assail a man until he has lifted himself above the lusting impulses. Temptation is an appeal to the impure. That which is pure cannot be subject to temptation.

Temptation waylays the man of aspiration until he touches the region of the divine consciousness, and beyond that border temptation cannot follow him. It is when a man begins to aspire that he begins to be tempted. Aspiration rouses up all the latent good and evil, in order that the man may be fully revealed to himself, for a man cannot overcome himself unless he fully knows himself.

It can scarcely be said of the merely animal man that he is tempted, for the very presence of temptation means that there is a striving for a purer state. Animal desire and gratification is the normal condition of the man who has not yet risen into aspiration. He wishes for nothing more, nothing better, than his sensual enjoyments, and is, for the present, satisfied. Such a man cannot be tempted to fall, for he has not yet risen.

The presence of aspiration signifies that a man has taken one step, at least, upward, and is therefore capable of being drawn back. This backward attraction is called temptation. The allurements of temptation subsist in the impure thoughts and downward desires of the heart. The object of temptation is powerless to attract when the heart no longer lusts for it. The stronghold of temptation is within a man, not without; and until a man realizes this, the period of temptation will be prolonged.

While a man continues to run away from outward objects, under the delusion that temptation subsists entirely in them, and does not attack and purge away his impure imaginings, his temptations will increase, and his falls will be many and grievous. When a man clearly perceives that the evil is within and not without, then his progress will be rapid, his temptations will decrease, and the final overcoming of all temptation will be well within the range of his spiritual vision.

Temptation is torment. It is not an abiding condition, but is a passage from a lower condition to a higher. The fullness and perfection of life is bliss, not torment. Temptation accompanies weakness and defeat, but a man is destined for strength and victory. The presence of torment is the signal to rise and conquer. The man of persistent and ever renewed aspiration does not allow himself to think that temptation cannot be overcome. He is determined to be master of himself. Resignation to evil is an acknowledgment of defeat. It signifies that the battle against self is abandoned; that good is denied; that evil is made supreme.

As the energetic man of business is not daunted by difficulties but studies how to overcome them, so the man of ceaseless aspiration is not crushed into submission by temptations, but meditates how he may fortify his mind. For the tempter is like a coward: he only creeps in at weak and unguarded points.

The tempted one should study thoughtfully the nature and meaning of temptation, for until it is known it cannot be overcome. A wise general, before attacking the opposing force, studies the tactics of his enemy. Likewise, he who is to overcome temptation must understand how it arises in his own darkness and error, and must study, by introspection and meditation, how to disperse the darkness and supplant error by truth.

The stronger a man's passions, the fiercer will be his temptations; the deeper his selfishness, the more subtle his temptations; the more pronounced his vanity, the more flattering and deceptive his temptations.

A man must know himself if he is to know the truth. He must not shrink from any revelation which will expose his error. On the contrary, he must welcome such revelations as aids to that self-knowledge which is the handmaid of self-conquest.

The man who cannot endure to have his errors and shortcomings brought to the surface and made known, but tries to hide them, is unfit to walk the highway of truth. He is not properly equipped to battle with and overcome temptation. He who cannot fearlessly face his lower nature, cannot climb the rugged heights of renunciation.

Let the tempted one know this: that he himself is both tempter and tempted; that all his enemies are within; that the flatterers which seduce, the taunts which stab, and the flames which burn, all spring from that inner region of ignorance and error in which he has hitherto lived. Knowing this, let him be assured of complete victory over evil. When he is sorely tempted, let him not mourn, therefore, but let him rejoice in that his strength is tried and his weaknesses exposed. For he who truly knows and humbly acknowledges his weakness will not be slow in setting about the acquisition of strength.

Foolish men blame others for their lapses and sins, but let the truth-lover blame only himself. Let him acknowledge his complete responsibility for his own conduct and not say, when he falls, this thing, or such and such a circumstance, or that man was to blame. For the most which others can do is to afford an opportunity for our own good or evil to manifest itself. They cannot make us good or evil.

Temptation is at first sore, grievous, and hard to be borne, and subtle and persistent is the assailant. But if the tempted one is firm and courageous, and does not give way, he will gradually subdue his spiritual enemy, and will finally triumph in the knowledge of good.

The adverse one is compounded of a man's own lust, selfishness, and pride. When these are put away, evil is seen to be naught, and good is revealed in all-victorious splendor.

12

THE USES OF TEMPTATION

The soul, in its journey towards perfection, passes through three distinct stages. The first is the animal stage, in which the man is content to live, in the gratification of his senses, unawakened to the knowledge of sin, or of his divine inheritance, and altogether unconscious of the spiritual possibilities within himself.

The second is the dual stage, in which the mind is continually oscillating between its animal and divine tendencies having become awakened to the consciousness of both. It is during this stage that temptation plays its part in the progress of the soul. It is a stage of continual fighting, of falling and rising, of sinning and repenting, for the man, still loving, and reluctant to leave, the gratifications in which he has so long lived, yet also aspires to the purity and excellence of the spiritual state, and he is continually mortified by an undecided choice.

Urged on by the divine life within him, this stage becomes at last one of deep anguish and suffering, and then the soul is ushered into the third stage, that of knowledge, in which the man rises above both sin and temptation, and enters into peace.

Temptation, like contentment in sin, is not a lasting condition, as the majority of people suppose; it is a passing phase, an experience through which the soul must pass; but as to whether a man will pass through that condition in this present life, and realise holiness and heavenly rest here and now, will depend entirely upon the strength of his intellectual and spiritual exertions, and upon the intensity and ardour with which he searches for Truth.

Temptation, with all its attendant torments can be overcome here and now, but it can only be overcome by knowledge. It is a condition of darkness or of semi-darkness. The fully enlightened soul is proof against all temptation. When a man fully understands the source, nature, and meaning of temptation, in that hour he will conquer it, and will rest from his long travail; but whilst he remains in ignorance, attention to religious observances, and much praying and reading of Scripture will fail to bring him peace.

If a man goes out to conquer an enemy, knowing nothing of his enemy's strength, tactics, or place of ambush, he will not only ignominiously fail, but will speedily fall into the hands of the enemy. He who would overcome his enemy the tempter, must discover his stronghold and place of concealment, and must also find out the unguarded gates in his own fortress where his enemy effects so easy an entrance. This necessitates continual meditation, ceaseless watchfulness, and constant and rigid introspection which lays bare, before the spiritual eyes of the tempted one, the vain and selfish motives of his soul. This is the holy warfare of the saints; it is the fight upon which every soul enters when it awakens out of its long sleep of animal indulgence.

Men fail to conquer, and the fight is indefinitely prolonged, because they labour, almost universally, under two delusions: first, that all temptations come from without; and second, that they are tempted because of their goodness. Whilst a man is held in bondage by these two delusions, he will make no progress; when he has shaken them off, he will pass on rapidly from victory to victory, and will taste of spiritual joy and rest.

Two searching truths must take the place of these two delusions, and those truths are: first, that all temptation comes from within; and second, that a man is tempted because of the evil that is within him. The idea that God, a devil, evil spirits, or outward objects are the source of temptation must be dispelled. The source and cause of all temptation is in the inward desire; that being purified or eliminated, outward objects and extraneous powers are utterly powerless to move the soul to sin or to temptation. The outward object is merely the occasion of the temptation, never the cause; this is in the desire of the one tempted. If the cause existed in the object, all men would be tempted alike, temptation could never be overcome, and men would be hopelessly doomed to endless torment; but seated, as it is, in his own desires, he has the remedy in his own hands, and can become victorious over all temptation by purifying those desires. A man is tempted because there are within him certain desires or states of mind which he has come to regard as unholy. These desires may lie asleep for a long time, and the man may think that he has got rid of them, when suddenly, on the presentation of an outward object, the sleeping desire wakes up and thirsts of immediate gratification; and this is the state of temptation.

The good in a man is never tempted. Goodness destroys temptation. It is the evil in a man that is aroused and tempted. The measure of a man's temptations is the exact register of his own unholiness. As a man purifies his heart, temptation ceases, for when a certain unlawful desire has been taken out of the heart, the object which formerly appealed to it can no longer do so, but becomes dead and powerless, for there is nothing left in the heart that can respond to it. The honest man cannot be tempted to steal, let the occasion be ever so opportune; the man of purified appetites cannot be tempted to gluttony and drunkenness, though the viands and wines be the most luscious; he of an enlightened understanding, whose mind is calm in the strength of inward virtue, can never be tempted to anger, irritability or revenge, and the wiles and charms of the wanton fall upon the purified heart as empty meaningless shadows.

Temptation shows a man just where he is sinful and ignorant, and is a means of urging him on to higher altitudes of knowledge and purity. Without temptation the soul cannot grow and become strong, there could be no wisdom, no real virtue; and though there would be lethargy and death, there could be no peace and no fullness of life. When temptation is understood and conquered, perfection is assured, and such perfection may become any man's who is willing to cast every selfish and impure desire by which he is possessed, into the sacrificial fire of knowledge. Let men, therefore, search diligently for Truth, realising that whilst they are subject to temptation, they have not comprehended Truth, and have much to learn.

Ye who are tempted know, then, that ye are tempted of yourselves. "For every man is tempted when he is drawn away of his own lusts," says the Apostle James. You are tempted because you are clinging to the animal within you and are unwilling to let go; because you are living in the false mortal self which is ever devoid of all true knowledge, knowing nothing, seeking nothing, but its own immediate gratification, ignorant of every Truth, and of every divine Principle. Clinging to that self, you continually suffer the pains of three separate torments; the torment of desire, the torment of repletion, and the torment of remorse.

> "So flameth Trishna, lust and thirst of things.
> Eager, ye cleave to shadows, dote on dreams;
> A false self in the midst ye plant, and make
> A World around which seems;
> Blind to the height beyond; deaf to the sound

Of sweet airs breathed from far past Indra's sky;
Dumb to the summons of the true life kept
For him who false puts by,
So grow the strifes and lusts which make earth's war,
So grieve poor cheated hearts and flow salt tears;
So wax the passions, envies, angers, hates;
So years chase blood-stained years
With wild red feet."

In that false self lies the germ of every suffering, the blight of every hope, the substance of every grief. When you are ready to give it up; when you are willing to have laid bare before you all its selfishness, impurity, and ignorance, and to confess its darkness to the uttermost, then will you enter upon the life of self- knowledge and self-mastery; you will become conscious of the god within you, of that divine nature which, seeking no gratification, abides in a region of perpetual joy and peace where suffering cannot come and where temptation can find no foothold. Establishing yourself, day by day, more and more firmly in that inward Divinity, the time will at last come when you will be able to say with Him whom millions worship, few understand and fewer still follow,—"The Prince of this world cometh and hath nothing in me."

13

THE OVERCOMING OF SELF

Many people have very confused and erroneous ideas concerning the terms "the overcoming of self", "the eradication of desire", and "the annihilation of the personality." Some (particularly the intellectual who are prone to theories) regard it as a metaphysical theory altogether apart from life and conduct; while others conclude that it is the crushing out of all life, energy and action, and the attempt to idealise stagnation and death. These errors and confusions, arising as they do in the minds of individuals, can only be removed by the individuals themselves; but perhaps it may make their removal a little less difficult (for those who are seeking Truth) by presenting the matter in another way.

The doctrine of the overcoming or annihilation of self is simplicity itself; indeed, so simple, practical, and close at hand is it that a child of five, whose mind has not yet become clouded with theories, theological schemes and speculative philosophies, would be far more likely to comprehend it than many older people who have lost their hold upon simple and beautiful truths by the adoption of complicated theories.

The annihilation of self consists in weeding out and destroying all those elements in the soul which lead to division, strife, suffering, disease and sorrow. It does not mean the destruction of any good and beautiful and peace-producing quality. For instance, when a man is tempted to irritability or anger, and by a great effort overcomes the selfish tendency, casts it from him, and acts from the spirit of patience and love, in that moment of self-conquest he practises the annihilation of self. Every noble man practises it in part, though he may deny it in his words, and he who carries out this practice to its completion, eradicating every selfish tendency until only the divinely beautiful qualities remain, he is said to have annihilated the personality (all the personal elements) and to have arrived at Truth. The self which is to be annihilated is composed of the following ten worthless and sorrow-producing elements:

- Lust
- Hatred
- Avarice
- Self-indulgence
- Self-seeking
- Vanity
- Pride
- Doubt
- Dark belief
- Delusion

It is the total abandonment, the complete annihilation of these ten elements, for they comprise the body of desire. On the other hand it teaches the cultivation, practice, and preservation of the following ten divine qualities:

- Purity
- Patience
- Humility
- Self-sacrifice
- Self-reliance
- Fearlessness
- Knowledge

- Wisdom
- Compassion
- Love

These comprise the Body of Truth, and to live entirely in them is to be a doer and knower of the Truth, is to be an embodiment of Truth. The combination of the ten elements is called Self or the Personality; the combination of the ten qualities produces what is called Truth; the Impersonal; the abiding, real and immortal Man.

It will thus be seen that it is not the destruction of any noble, true, and enduring quality that is taught, but only the destruction of those things that are ignoble, false and evanescent. Neither is this overcoming of self the deprivation of gladness, happiness and joy, but rather is it the constant possession of these things by living in the joy-begetting qualities. It is the abandonment of the lust for enjoyment, but not of enjoyment itself; the destruction of the *thirst* for pleasure, but not of pleasure itself; the annihilation of the *selfish longing* for love, and power, and possessions themselves. It is the preservation of all those things which draw and bind men together in unity and concord, and, far from idealising stagnation and death, urges men to the practice of those qualities which lead to the highest, noblest, most effective, and enduring action. He whose actions proceed from some or all of the ten elements wastes his energies upon negations, and does not preserve his soul; but he whose actions proceed from some or all of the ten qualities, he truly and wisely acts and so preserves his soul.

He who lives largely in the ten earthly elements, and who is blind and deaf to the spiritual verities, will find no attraction in the doctrine of self-surrender, for it will appear to him as the complete extinction of his being; but he who is endeavouring to live in the ten heavenly qualities will see the glory and beauty of the doctrine, and will know it as the foundation of Life Eternal. He will also see that when men apprehend and practise it, industry, commerce, government, and every worldly activity will be purified; and action, purpose and intelligence, instead of being destroyed, will be intensified and enlarged, but freed from strife and pain.

14

THE SCIENCE OF SELF-CONTROL

We live in a scientific age. Men of science are numbered by thousands, and they are ceaselessly searching, analyzing, and experimenting with a view to discovery and the increase of knowledge.

The shelves of our libraries, both public and private, are heavy with their load of imposing volumes on scientific subjects, and the wonderful achievements of modern science are always before us—whether in our homes or in our streets, in country or town, on land or sea—there shall we have before us some marvelous device, some recent accomplishment of science, for adding to our comfort, increasing our speed, or saving the labor of our hands.

Yet, with all our vast store of scientific knowledge, and its startling and rapidly increasing results in the world of discovery and invention, there is, in this age, one branch of science which has so far fallen into decay as to have become almost forgotten; a science, nevertheless, which is of greater importance than all the other sciences combined, and without which all science would but subserve the ends of selfishness, and aid in man's destruction—I refer to the Science of Self-control.

Our modern scientists study the elements and forces which are outside themselves, with the object of controlling and utilizing them. The ancients studied the elements and forces which were within themselves, with a view to controlling and utilizing them, and the ancients produced such mighty Masters of knowledge in this direction, that to this day they are held in reverence as gods, and the vast religious organizations of the world are based upon their achievements.

Wonderful as are the forces in nature, they are vastly inferior to that combination of intelligent forces which comprise the mind of man, and which dominate and direct the blind mechanical forces of nature. Therefore, it follows that, to understand, control, and direct the inner forces of passion, desire, will, and intellect, is to be in possession of the destinies of men and nations.

As in ordinary science, there are, in this divine science, degrees of attainment; and a man is great in knowledge, great in himself, and great in his influence on the world, in the measure that he is great in self-control.

He who understands and dominates the forces of external nature is the natural scientist; but he who understands and dominates the internal forces of the mind is the divine scientist; and the laws which operate in gaining a knowledge of external appearances, operate also in gaining a knowledge of internal varieties.

A man cannot become an accomplished scientist in a few weeks or months, nay, not even in a few years. But only after many years of painstaking investigation can he speak with authority, and be ranked among the masters of science. Likewise, a man cannot acquire self-control, and become possessed of the wisdom and peace giving knowledge which that self-control confers, but by many years of patient labor; a labor which is all the more arduous because it is silent, and both unrecognized and unappreciated by others; and he who would pursue this science successfully must learn to stand alone, and to toil unrewarded, as far as any outward emolument is concerned.

The natural scientist pursues, in acquiring his particular

kind of knowledge, the following five orderly and sequential steps:

1. Observation: that is, he closely and persistently observes the facts of nature.

2. Experiment: Having become acquainted, by repeated observations, with certain facts, he experiments with those facts, with a view to the discovery of natural laws. He puts his facts through rigid processes of analysis, and so finds out what is useless and what of value; and he rejects the former and retains the latter.

3. Classification: Having accumulated and verified a mass of facts by numberless observations and experiments, he commences to classify those facts, to arrange them in orderly groups with the object of discovering some underlying law, some hidden and unifying principle, which governs, regulates, and binds together these facts.

4. Deduction: Thus he passes on to the fourth step of deduction. From the facts and results which are before him, he discovers certain invariable modes of action, and thus reveals the hidden laws of things.

5. Knowledge: Having proven and established certain laws, it may be said of such a man that he knows. He is a scientist, a man of knowledge.

But the attainment of scientific knowledge is not the end, great as it is. Men do not attain knowledge for themselves alone, nor to keep it locked secretly in their hearts, like a beautiful jewel in a dark chest. The end of such knowledge is use, service, the increase of the comfort and happiness of the world. Thus, when a man has become a scientist, he gives the world the benefit of his knowledge, and unselfishly bestows upon mankind the results of all his labors.

Thus, beyond knowledge, there is a further step of Use: that is, the right and unselfish use of the knowledge acquired; the application of knowledge to invention for the common weal.

It will be noted that the five steps or processes enumerated follow in orderly succession, and that no man can become a scientist who omits any one of them. Without the first step of systematic observation, for instance, he could not even enter the realm of knowledge of nature's secrets.

At first, the searcher for such knowledge has before him a universe of things: these things he does not understand; many of them, indeed, seem to be irreconcilably opposed one to the other, and there is apparent confusion; but by patiently and laboriously pursuing these five processes, he discovers the order, nature, and essences of things; perceives the central law or laws which bind them together in harmonious relationship, and so puts an end to confusion and ignorance.

As with the natural scientist, so with the divine scientist; he must pursue, with the same self-sacrificing diligence, five progressive steps in the attainment of self-knowledge, self-control. These five steps are the same as with the natural scientist, but the process is reversed, the mind, instead of being centered upon external things, is turned back upon itself, and the investigations are pursued in the realm of mind (of one's own mind) instead of in that of matter.

At first, the searcher for divine knowledge is confronted with that mass of desires, passions, emotions, ideas, and intellections which he calls himself, which is the basis of all his actions, and from which his life proceeds.

This combination of invisible, yet powerful, forces appears confusedly; some of them stand, apparently, in direct conflict with each other, without any appearance or hope of reconciliation;

his mind in its entirety, too, with his life which proceeds from that mind, does not seem to have any equitable relation to many other minds and lives about him, and altogether there is a condition of pain and confusion from which he would fain escape.

Thus, he begins by keenly realizing his state of ignorance, for no one could acquire either natural or divine knowledge, if he were convinced that without study or labor he already possessed it.

With such perception of one's ignorance, there comes the desire for knowledge, and the novice in self-control enters upon the ascending pathway, in which are the following five steps:

1. **Introspection:** This coincides with the observation of the natural scientist. The mental eye is turned like a searchlight upon the inner things of the mind, and its subtle and ever varying processes are observed and carefully noted. This stepping aside from selfish gratifications, from the excitements of worldly pleasures and ambitions, in order to observe, with the object of understanding, one's nature, is the beginning of self-control. Hitherto, the man has been blindly and impotently borne along by the impulses of his nature, the mere creature of things and circumstances, but now he puts a check upon his impulses and, instead of being controlled, begins to control.

2. **Self-analysis:** Having observed the tendencies of the mind, they are then closely examined, and are put through a rigid process of analysis. The evil tendencies (those that produce painful effects) are separated from the good tendencies (those that produce peaceful effects); and the various tendencies, with the particular actions they produce, and the definite results which invariably spring from these

actions, are gradually grasped by the understanding, which is at last enabled to follow them in their swift and subtle interplay and profound ramifications. It is a process of testing and proving, and, for the searcher, a period of being tested and proved.

3. **Adjustment:** By this time, the practical student of things divine has clearly before him every tendency and aspect of his nature, down to the profoundest promptings of his mind, and the most subtle motives of his heart. There is not a spot or corner left, which he has not explored and illuminated with the light of self-examination.

    He is familiar with every weak and selfish point, every strong and virtuous quality. It is considered the height of wisdom to be able to see ourselves as others see us, but the practitioner of self-control goes far beyond this: he not only sees himself as others see him, he sees himself as he is. Thus, standing face to face with himself, not striving to hide away from any secret fault; no longer defending himself with pleasant flatteries; neither underrating nor overrating himself or his powers, and no more cursed with self-praise or self-pity, he sees the full magnitude of the task which lies before him; sees dearly ahead the heights of self-control, and knows what work he has to do to reach them.

    He is no longer in a state of confusion, but has gained a glimpse of the laws which operate in the world of thought, and he now begins to adjust his mind in accordance with those laws. This is a process of weeding, sifting, cleansing. As the farmer weeds, cleans, and prepares the ground for his crops, so the student removes the weeds of evil from his mind, cleanses and purifies it preparatory to sowing the seeds of righteous actions which shall produce the harvest of a well ordered life.

4. **Righteousness:** Having adjusted his thoughts and deeds to those minor laws which operate in mental activities in the production of pain and pleasure, unrest and peace, sorrow and bliss, he now perceives that there is involved in those laws one Great Central Law which, like the law of gravitation in the natural world, is supreme in the world of mind; a law to which all thoughts and deeds are subservient, and by which they are regulated and kept in their proper sphere.

   This is the law of Justice or Righteousness, which is universal and supreme. To this law he now conforms. Instead of thinking and acting blindly, as the nature is stimulated and appealed to by outward things, he subordinates his thoughts and deeds to this central principle. He no longer acts from self, but does what is right—what is universally and eternally right. He is no longer the abject slave of his nature and circumstances, he is the master of his nature and circumstances.

   He is no longer carried hither and thither on the forces of his mind; he controls and guides those forces to the accomplishment of his purposes. Thus, having his nature in control and subjection, not thinking thoughts nor doing deeds which oppose the righteous law, and which, therefore, that law annuls with suffering and defeat, he rises above the dominion of sin and sorrow, ignorance and doubt, and is strong, calm, and peaceful.

5. **Pure Knowledge:** By thinking right and acting right, he proves, by experience, the existence of the divine law on which the mind is framed, and which is the guiding and unifying principle in all human affairs and events, whether individual or national. Thus, by perfecting himself in self-control, he acquires divine knowledge; he reaches the point

where it may be said of him, as of the natural scientist, that he knows.

He has mastered the science of self-control, and has brought knowledge out of ignorance, order out of confusion. He has acquired that knowledge of self which includes knowledge of all men; that knowledge of one's own life which embraces knowledge of all live—as for all minds are the same in essence (differing only in degree), are framed upon the same law; and the same thoughts and acts, by whatsoever individual they are wrought, will always produce the same results.

But this divine and peace bestowing knowledge, as in the case of the natural scientist, is not gained for one's self alone; for if this were so, the aim of evolution would be frustrated, and it is not in the nature of things to fall short of ripening and accomplishment; and, indeed, he who thought to gain this knowledge solely for his own happiness would most surely fail.

So, beyond the fifth step of Pure Knowledge, there is a still further one of Wisdom, which is the right application of the knowledge acquired; the pouring out upon the world, unselfishly and without stint, the result of one's labors, thus accelerating progress and uplifting humanity.

It may be said of men who have not gone back into their own nature to control and purify it, that they cannot clearly distinguish between good and evil, right and wrong. They reach after those things which they think will give them pleasure, and try to avoid those things which they believe will cause them pain.

The source of their actions is self, and they only discover right painfully and in a fragmentary way, by periodically passing through severe sufferings, and lashings of conscience. But he who practices self-control, passing through the five processes, which are five stages of growth, gains that knowledge which enables him to act from the moral law which sustains the universe. He knows good and evil, right and wrong, and, thus knowing them, lives in accordance with good and right. He no longer needs to consider what is pleasant or what is unpleasant, but does what is right; his nature is in harmony with his conscience, and there is no remorse; his mind is in unison with the Great Law, and there is no more suffering and sin; for him evil is ended, and good is all in all.

15

RIGHT THINKING AND REPOSE

Life is a Combination of Habits, some baneful, some beneficent, all of which take their rise in the one habit of thinking. The thought makes the man; therefore right-thinking is the most important thing in life. The essential difference between a wise man and a fool is that the wise man controls his thinking, the fool is controlled by it. A wise man determines how and what he shall think, and does not allow external things to divert his thought from the main purpose. But a fool is carried captive by every tyrant thought as it is aroused within him by external things, and he goes through life the helpless tool of impulse, whim, and passion.

Careless, slovenly thinking, commonly called thoughtlessness, is the companion of failure, wrongdoing, and wretchedness. Nothing, no prayers, no religious ceremonies, not even acts of charity, can make up for wrong-thinking. Only right-thinking can rectify a wrong life. Only the right attitude of mind towards men and things can bring repose and peace.

The Triumphant Life is only for him whose heart and intellect are attuned to lofty virtue. He must make his thought logical, sequential, harmonious, symmetrical. He must mold and shape his thinking to fixed principles, and thereby establish his life on the sure foundation of knowledge. He must not merely be kind, he must be intelligently kind; must know why he is kind. His kindness must be an invariable quality, and not an intermittent impulse interspersed with fits of resentment and acts of harshness. He must not merely be virtuous under virtuous circumstances; his virtue must be of a kind that shall continue to shine with unabated light when he is assailed with vicious circumstances. He must not allow himself to be hurled from the throne of divine manhood by the shocks of fate or the praise and blame of those around him. Virtue must be his abiding habitation; his refuge from the whirlwind and the storm.

And virtue is not only of the heart; it is of the intellect also; and without this virtue of the intellect, the virtue of the heart is imperiled. Reason, like passion, has its vices. Metaphysical speculations are the riot of the intellect, as sensuality is the riot of the affections. The highest flights of speculation—pleasing as they are—reveal no place of rest, and the strained mind must return to facts and moral principles to find that truth which it seeks. As the soaring bird returns for refuge and rest to its nest in the rock, so must the speculative thinker return to the rock of virtue for surety and peace.

The intellect must be trained to comprehend the principles of virtue, and to understand all that is involved in their practice. Its energies must be restrained from wasteful indulgence in vain subtleties, and be directed in the path of righteousness and the way of wisdom. The thinker must distinguish, in his own mind, between reality and assumption. He must discover the extent of his actual knowledge. He must know what he knows. He must also know what he does not know. He must learn to discriminate between belief and knowledge, error and Truth.

In his search for the right attitude of mind which perceives truth, and works out a wise and radiant life, he must be more logical than logic, more merciless in exposing the errors of his own mind than the most sarcastic logician is in exposing the errors of the minds of others. After pursuing this course of discrimination for a short time, he will be astonished to find how small is the extent of his actual knowledge; yet he will be gladdened by its possession, for small as it is, it is the pure gold of knowledge. And what is better, to have a few grains of gold hidden away in tons of ore, where it is useless, or to extract the gold and throw away the ore?

As the miner sifts away bushels of dull earth to find the sparkling diamond, so the spiritual miner, the true thinker, sifts away from his mind the accumulation of opinions, beliefs, speculations, and assumptions to find the bright jewel of Truth which bestows upon its possessor wisdom and enlightenment.

And the concentrated knowledge which is ultimately brought to light by this sifting process is found to be so closely akin to virtue that it cannot be divided from it, cannot be set apart as something different.

In his search for knowledge Socrates discovered virtue. The divine maxims of the Great Teachers are maxims of virtue. When knowledge is separated from virtue, wisdom is lost. What a man practices, that he knows. What he does not practice, that he does not know. A man may write treatises or preach sermons on Love, but if he treats his family harshly, or thinks spitefully of his enemy, what knowledge has he concerning Love?

In the heart of the man of knowledge there dwells a silent and abiding compassion that shames the fine words of the noisy theorist. He only knows what peace is whose heart is free from hatred, who lives in peace with all. Cunning definitions of virtue only serve to deepen ignorance when they proceed from vice-stained lips. Knowledge has a deeper source than the mere memorizing of information. That knowledge is divine which proceeds from acquaintance with virtue. The humility which purges the intellect of its empty opinions and vain assumptions also fortifies it with a searching insight and invincible power.

There is a divine logic which is indistinguished from love. The reply, "He that is without sin among you, let him cast the first stone," is unanswerable logic. It is also perfect love.

The wrong thinker is known by his vices; the right thinker is know by his virtues. Troubles and unrest assail the mind of the wrong thinker, and he experiences no abiding repose. He imagines that others can injure, snub, cheat, degrade and ruin him. Knowing nothing of the protection of virtue, he seeks the protection of self, and takes refuge in suspicion, spite, resentment, and retaliation, and is burnt in the fire of his own vices.

When slandered, he slanders in return; when accused, he recriminates; when assailed, he turns upon his adversary with double fierceness. "I have been treated unjustly!" exclaims the wrong thinker, and then abandons himself to resentment and misery. Having no insight and unable to distinguish evil from good, he cannot see that his own evil, and not his neighbor's, is the cause of all his trouble.

The right thinker is not concerned with thoughts about self and self-protection, and the wrong actions of others towards him cannot cause him trouble or unrest. He cannot think— "This man has wronged me." He perceives that no wrong can reach him but by his own evil deeds. He understands that his welfare is at his own hands, and thus none but himself can rob him of repose. Virtue is his protection, and retaliation is foreign to him. He holds himself steadfastly in peace, and resentment cannot enter his heart. Temptation does not find him unprepared, and it assails in vain the strong citadel of his mind. Abiding in virtue, he abides in strength and peace.

The right-thinker has discovered and acquired the right attitude of mind toward men and things—the attitude of a profound and loving repose. And this is not resignation, it is wisdom. It is not indifference, but watchful and penetrating insight. He has comprehended the facts of life; he sees things as they are. He does not overlook the particulars of life, but reads them in the light of cosmic law; sees them in their right relations as portions of the universal scheme. He sees the universe is upheld by justice. He watches, but does not engage in, the petty quarrels and fleeting strifes of men. He cannot be partisan. His sympathy is with all. He cannot favor one portion more than another. He knows that good will ultimately conquer in the world, as it has conquered in individuals; that there is a sense in which good already conquers, for evil defeats itself.

Good is not defeated; justice is not set aside. Whatever man may do, justice reigns, and its eternal throne cannot be assailed and threatened, much less conquered and overthrown. This is the source of the true thinker's abiding repose. Having become righteous, he perceives the righteous law. Having acquired Love, he understands the Eternal Love. Having conquered evil, he knows that good is supreme.

He is only the true thinker whose heart is free from hatred, lust, and pride; who looks out upon the world through eyes washed free from evil; whose bitterest enemy arouses no enmity, but only tender pity in his heart; who does not talk vainly about things of which he has no knowledge, and whose heart is always at peace.

And by this a man may know that his thoughts are in accordance with the Truth—that there is no more bitterness in his heart, that malice has departed from him; that he loves where he formerly condemned.

A man may be learned, but if he is not wise he will not be a true thinker. Not by learning will a man triumph over evil; not by much study will he overcome sin and sorrow. Only by conquering himself will he conquer evil; only by practicing righteousness will he put an end to sorrow.

Not for the clever, nor the learned, nor the self-confident is the Life Triumphant, but for the pure, the virtuous, the wise. The former achieve their particular success in life, but the latter alone achieve the Great Success, a success so invincible and complete that even an apparent defeat shines with added victory.

Virtue cannot be shaken; virtue cannot be confounded; virtue cannot be overthrown. He who thinks in accordance with virtue, who acts righteously, whose mind is the servant of truth, he it is who conquers in life and in death. For virtue must triumph, and Righteousness and Truth are the pillars of the universe.

16

TRANSCENDENCE

When a man passes from the dark stage of temptation to the more enlightened stage of transmutation, he has become a saint. A saint is one who perceives the need for self-purification, who understands the way of self-purification, and who has entered that way and is engaged in perfecting himself.

But there comes a time in the process of transmutation when, with the decrease of evil and the accumulation of good, there dawns in the mind a new vision, a new consciousness, a new man. When this is reached, the saint has become a sage; he has passed from the human life to the divine life. He is "born again," and there begins for him a new round of experiences. He wields a new power; a new universe opens out before his spiritual gaze. This is the stage of transcendence. This I call the Transcendent Life.

When there is no more consciousness of sin; when anxiety and doubt, and grief and sorrow, are ended; when lust and animosity, and anger and envy, no more possess the thoughts; when there remains in the mind no vestige of blame towards others for one's own condition, and when all conditions are seen to be good because they are the result of causes, so that no event can afflict the mind, then Transcendence is attained. Then the limited personality is outgrown, and the divine life is known; evil is transcended, and Good is all-in-all.

The divine consciousness is not an intensification of the human; it is a new form of consciousness. It springs from the old, but it is not a continuance of it. Born of the lower life of sin and sorrow, after a period of painful torment, it yet transcends that life and has no part in it, just as the perfect flower transcends the seed from which it sprang.

As passion is the keynote of the self-life, so serenity is the keynote of the transcendent life. Rising into it, man is lifted above disharmony and disturbance. When Perfect Good is realized and known, not as an opinion or an idea, but as an experience or a possession, then calm vision is acquired, and tranquil joy abides through all hardships.

The Transcendent Life is ruled, not by passions, but by principles. It is founded not upon fleeting impulses, but upon abiding laws. In its clear atmosphere the orderly sequence of all things is revealed, so that there is seen to be no room for sorrow, anxiety, or regret.

While men are involved in the passions of self, they burden themselves with cares, and trouble themselves over many things. Above all else, they trouble over their own little, burdened, pain-stricken personality, being anxious for its fleeting pleasures, for its protection and preservation, and for its eternal safety and continuance. Now in the life that is wise and good all this is transcended. Personal interests are replaced by universal purposes, and all cares, troubles, and anxieties concerning the pleasure and the fate of the personality are dispelled like the feverish dreams of a night.

Passion is blind and ignorant. It sees and knows only its own gratification. Self recognizes no law; its object is to get and to enjoy. The getting is a graduated scale varying from sensual greed, through many subtle vanities, up to the desire for a personal heaven or personal immortality, but it is self still. It is the old sensual craving coming out in a more subtle and deceptive form. It is longing for some personal delight, along with its accompanying fear that delight should be lost forever.

In the transcendent state, desire and dread are ended, and the thirst for gain and the fear of loss are things that are no more. For where the universal order is seen, and where perennial joy in that good is a normal condition, what is there left to desire? What remains to be feared?

He who has brought his entire nature into conformity and harmony with the law of righteousness, who has made his thoughts pure and his deeds blameless, has entered liberty. He has transcended darkness and mortality, and has passed into light and immortality. For the transcendent state is at first a higher order of morality, then a new form of perception, and at last a comprehensive understanding of the universal moral causation. And this morality, this vision, and this understanding constitute the new consciousness, the divine life.

The transcendent man is he who is above and beyond the dominion of self. He has transcended evil and lives in the practice and knowledge of good. He is like a man who, having long looked upon the world with darkened eyes, is now restored to sight, and sees things as they are.

Evil is an experience, and not a power. If it were an independent power in the universe, it could not be transcended by any being. But though not real as a power, it is real as a condition and an experience, for all experience is of the nature of reality. It is a state of ignorance, of undevelopment and as such it recedes and disappears before the light of knowledge, as the intellectual ignorance of a child vanishes before the gradually accumulating learning, or as darkness dissolves before the rising light.

The painful experiences of evil pass away as the new experiences of good enter into and possess the field of consciousness. And what are the new experiences of good?

They are many and beautiful—such as the joyful knowledge of the freedom from sin. They are the absence of remorse and deliverance from all torments of temptation. They are ineffable joy in conditions and circumstances which formerly caused deep affliction, and imperviousness to be hurt by the actions of others. They are great patience and sweetness of character; serenity of mind under all circumstances; and emancipation from doubt, fear, and anxiety. They are freedom from all dislike, envy, and animosity, with the power to feel and act kindly towards those who see fit to constitute themselves as one's enemies or opponents. They are the divine power to give blessings for curses, and to return good for evil; a deep knowledge of the human heart, with a perception of its fundamental goodness; and insight into the law of moral causation and the mental evolution of beings, with a prophetic foresight of the sublime good that awaits humanity. Above all, they are a glad rejoicing in the limitation and impotency of evil, and in the eternal supremacy and power of good.

All these, and the calm, strong, far-reaching life that these imply and contain, are the rich experiences of the transcendent man, along with all the new and varied resources, the vast powers, the quickened abilities, and enlarged capacities that spring to life in the new consciousness.

Transcendence is surpassing virtue. Evil and good cannot dwell together. Evil must be abandoned, left behind and transcended before good is grasped and known. When good is practiced and fully comprehended, then all the afflictions of the mind are at an end. For that which is accompanied with pain and sorrow in the consciousness of evil is not so accompanied in the consciousness of good.

Whatsoever happens to the good man cannot cause him perplexity or sorrow, for he knows its cause and issue, knows the good which it is ordained to accomplish in himself, and so his mind remains happy and serene. Though the body of the good man may be bound, his mind is free. Though it be wounded and in pain, joy and peace abide within his heart.

A spiritual teacher had a pupil who was apt and earnest. After several years of learning and practice, the pupil one day offered a question for discussion which his master could not answer. After days of deep meditation, the master said to his pupil, "I cannot answer the question which you have asked. Have you any solution to offer?" Whereupon the pupil formulated a reply to the question which he had propounded. The master then said to him: "You have answered that which I could not, and henceforth neither I nor any man can instruct you, for now you are indeed instructed by truth. You have soared, like the kingly eagle, where no man can follow. Your work is now to instruct others. You are no longer the pupil, you have become the master."

In looking back on the self-life which he has transcended, the divinely enlightened man sees all the afflictions of that life as though his schoolmasters were teaching and leading him upward. And in the measure that he penetrated their meaning and lifted himself above them, they departed from him. Their mission to teach him having ended, they left him the triumphant master of the field. For the lower cannot teach the higher; ignorance cannot instruct wisdom; evil cannot enlighten good; nor can the pupil set lessons for the master. That which is transcended cannot reach up to that which transcends. Evil can only teach in its own sphere, where it is regarded as master. In the sphere of good it has no place and no authority.

The strong traveler on the highway of truth knows no such thing as resignation to evil; he knows only obedience to good. He who submits to evil, saying, "Sin cannot be overcome, and evil must be borne," thereby acknowledges that evil is his master. It is not his master to instruct him, but to bind and oppress him. The lover of good cannot also be a lover of evil, nor can he, for one moment, admit its ascendancy. He elevates and glorifies good, not evil. He loves light, not darkness.

When a man makes truth his master, he abandons error. As he transcends error, he becomes more like his master, until at last he becomes one with truth, teaching it, as a master, by his actions, and reflecting it in his life.

Transcendence is not an abnormal condition; it belongs to the orderly process of evolution. Though, as yet, few have reached it, all will come into it in the course of the ages. And he who ascends into it sins no more, sorrows no more, and is no more troubled. Good are his thoughts, good are his actions, and the good is the tranquil tenor of his way. He has conquered self, and has submitted to truth. He has mastered evil, and has comprehended good. Henceforth neither men nor books can instruct him, for he is instructed by the Supreme Good, the spirit of truth.

17

THE SECRET OF
ABOUNDING HAPPINESS

Great is the thirst for happiness, and equally great is the lack of happiness. The majority of the poor long for riches, believing that their possession would bring them supreme and lasting happiness.

Many who are rich, having gratified every desire and whim, suffer from ennui and repletion, and are farther from the possession of happiness even than the very poor.

If we reflect upon this state of things it will ultimately lead us to a knowledge of the all important truth that happiness is not derived from mere outward possessions, nor misery from the lack of them; for if this were so, we should find the poor always miserable, and the rich always happy, whereas the reverse is frequently the case.

Some of the most wretched people whom I have known were those who were surrounded with riches and luxury, whilst some of the brightest and happiest people I have met were possessed of only the barest necessities of life.

Many men who have accumulated riches have confessed that the selfish gratification which followed the acquisition of riches has robbed life of its sweetness, and that they were never so happy as when they were poor.

What, then, is happiness, and how is it to be secured? Is it a figment, a delusion, and is suffering alone perennial?

We shall find, after earnest observation and reflection, that all, except those who have entered the way of wisdom, believe that happiness is only to be obtained by the gratification of desire.

It is this belief, rooted in the soil of ignorance, and continually watered by selfish cravings, that is the cause of all the misery in the world.

And I do not limit the word desire to the grosser animal cravings; it extends to the higher psychic realm, where far more powerful, subtle, and insidious cravings hold in bondage the intellectual and refined, depriving them of all that beauty, harmony, and purity of soul whose expression is happiness.

Most people will admit that selfishness is the cause of all the unhappiness in the world, but they fall under the soul-destroying delusion that it is somebody else's selfishness, and not their own.

When you are willing to admit that all your unhappiness is the result of your own selfishness you will not be far from the gates of Paradise; but so long as you are convinced that it is the selfishness of others that is robbing you of joy, so long will you remain a prisoner in your self-created purgatory.

Happiness is that inward state of perfect satisfaction which is joy and peace, and from which all desire is eliminated. The satisfaction which results from gratified desire is brief and illusionary, and is always followed by an increased demand for gratification.

Desire is as insatiable as the ocean, and clamors louder and louder as its demands are attended to.

It claims ever-increasing service from its deluded devotees, until at last they are struck down with physical or mental anguish, and are hurled into the purifying fires of suffering. Desire is the region of hell, and all torments are centered there.

The giving up of desire is the realization of heaven, and all delights await the pilgrim there,

> I sent my soul through the invisible,
> Some letter of that after life to spell,
> And by-and-by my soul returned to me,
> And whispered, I myself am heaven and hell,

Heaven and hell are inward states. Sink into self and all its gratifications, and you sink into hell; rise above self into that state of consciousness which is the utter denial and forgetfulness of self, and you enter heaven.

Self is blind, without judgment, not possessed of true knowledge, and always leads to suffering. Correct perception, unbiased judgment, and true knowledge belong only to the divine state, and only in so far as you realize this divine consciousness can you know what real happiness is.

So long as you persist in selfishly seeking for your own personal happiness, so long will happiness elude you, and you will be sowing the seeds of wretchedness.

In so far as you succeed in losing yourself in the service of others, in that measure will happiness come to you, and you will reap a harvest of bliss.

> It is in loving, not in being loved,
> The heart is blessed;
> It is in giving, not in seeking gifts,
> We find our quest.

> Whatever be thy longing or thy need,
> That do thou give;
> So shall thy soul be fed, and thou indeed
> Shalt truly live.

Cling to self, and you cling to sorrow, relinquish self, and you enter into peace. To seek selfishly is not only to lose happiness, but even that which we believe to be the source of happiness.

See how the glutton is continually looking about for a new delicacy wherewith to stimulate his deadened appetite; and how, bloated, burdened, and diseased, scarcely any food at last is eaten with pleasure.

Whereas, he who has mastered his appetite, and not only does not seek, but never thinks of gustatory pleasure, finds delight in the most frugal meal. The angel-form of happiness, which men, looking through the eyes of self, imagine they see in gratified desire, when clasped is always found to be the skeleton of misery. Truly, "He that seeketh his life shall lose it, and he that loseth his life shall find it."

Abiding happiness will come to you when, ceasing to selfishly cling, you are willing to give up. When you are willing to lose, unreservedly, that impermanent thing which is so dear to you, and which, whether you cling to it or not, will one day be snatched from you, then you will find that that which seemed to you like a painful loss, turns out to be a supreme gain.

To give up in order to gain, than this there is no greater delusion, nor no more prolific source of misery; but to be willing to yield up and to suffer loss, this is indeed the Way of Life.

How is it possible to find real happiness by centering ourselves in those things which, by their very nature, must pass away? Abiding and real happiness can only be found by centering ourselves in that which is permanent.

Rise, therefore, above the clinging to and the craving for impermanent things, and you will then enter into a consciousness of the Eternal, and as, rising above self, and by growing more and more into the spirit of purity, self-sacrifice and universal Love, you become centered in that consciousness, you will realize that happiness which has no reaction, and which can never be taken from you.

The heart that has reached utter self-forgetfulness in its love for others has not only become possessed of the highest happiness but has entered into immortality, for it has realized the Divine.

Look back upon your life, and you will find that the moments of supremest happiness were those in which you uttered some word, or performed some act, of compassion or self-denying love. Spiritually, happiness and harmony are, synonymous.

Harmony is one phase of the Great Law whose spiritual expression is love. All selfishness is discord, and to be selfish is to be out of harmony with the Divine order.

As we realize that all-embracing love which is the negation of self, we put ourselves in harmony with the divine music, the universal song, and that ineffable melody which is true happiness becomes our own.

Men and women are rushing hither and thither in the blind search for happiness, and cannot find it; nor ever will until they recognize that happiness is already within them and round about them, filling the universe, and that they, in their selfish searching are shutting themselves out from it.

> I followed happiness to make her mine,
> Past towering oak and swinging ivy vine.
> She fled, I chased, o'er slanting hill and dale,
> O'er fields and meadows, in the purpling vale;
> Pursuing rapidly o'er dashing stream.
> I scaled the dizzy cliffs where eagles scream;
> I traversed swiftly every land and M.
> But always happiness eluded me.

Exhausted, fainting, I pursued no more,
But sank to rest upon a barren shore.
One came and asked for food, and one for alms
I placed the bread and gold in bony palms.
One came for sympathy, and one for rest;
I shared with every needy one my best;
When, lo! sweet Happiness, with form divine,
Stood by me, whispering softly, 'I am thine'.

These beautiful lines of Burleigh's express the secret of all abounding happiness. Sacrifice the personal and transient, and you rise at once into the impersonal and permanent.

Give up that narrow cramped self that seeks to render all things subservient to its own petty interests, and you will enter into the company of the angels, into the very heart and essence of universal Love.

Forget yourself entirely in the sorrows of others and in ministering to others, and divine happiness will emancipate you from all sorrow and suffering.

"Taking the first step with a good thought, the second with a good word, and the third with a good deed, I entered Paradise." And you also may enter into Paradise by pursuing the same course. It is not beyond, it is here. It is realized only by the unselfish.

It is known in its fullness only to the pure in heart. If you have not realized this unbounded happiness you may begin to actualize it by ever holding before you the lofty ideal of unselfish love, and aspiring towards it.

Aspiration or prayer is desire turned upward. It is the soul turning toward its Divine source, where alone permanent satisfaction can be found. By aspiration the destructive forces of desire are transmuted into divine and all-preserving energy.

To aspire is to make an effort to shake off the trammels of desire; it is the prodigal made wise by loneliness and suffering, returning to his Father's Mansion.

As you rise above the sordid self; as you break, one after another, the chains that bind you, will you realize the joy of giving, as distinguished from the misery of grasping—giving of your substance; giving of your intellect; giving of the love and light that is growing within you.

You will then understand that it is indeed "more blessed to give than to receive." But the giving must be of the heart without any taint of self, without desire for reward. The gift of pure love is always attended with bliss. If, after you have given, you are wounded because you are not thanked or flattered, or your name put in the paper, know then that your gift was prompted by vanity and not by love, and you were merely giving in order to get; were not really giving, but grasping.

Lose yourself in the welfare of others; forget yourself in all that you do; this is the secret of abounding happiness.

Ever be on the watch to guard against selfishness, and learn faithfully the divine lessons of inward sacrifice; so shall you climb the highest heights of happiness, and shall remain in the neverclouded sunshine of universal joy, clothed in the shining garment of immortality.

Are you searching for the happiness that does not fade away?

Are you looking for the joy that lives, and leaves no grievous day?

Are you panting for the waterbrooks of Love, and Life, and Peace?

Then let all dark desires depart, and selfish seeking cease.

Are you ling'ring in the paths of pain, grief-haunted, stricken sore?

Are you wand'ring in the ways that wound your weary feet the more?

Are you sighing for the Resting-Place where tears and sorrows cease?

Then sacrifice your selfish heart and find the Heart of Peace.

18

HABIT: ITS SLAVERY AND ITS FREEDOM

Man is subject to the law of habit. Is he then free? Yes, he is free. Man did not make life and its laws; they are eternal; he finds himself involved in them and he can understand and obey them. Man's power does not enable him to make laws of being; it subsists in discrimination and choice. Man does not create one jot of the universal conditions or laws; they are the essential principles of things, and are neither made nor unmade. He discovers, not makes, them. Ignorance of them is at the root of the world's pain. To defy them is folly and bondage. Who is the freer man, the thief who defies the laws of his country or the honest citizen who obeys them? Who, again, is the freer man, the fool who thinks he can live as he likes, or the wise man who chooses to do only that which is right?

Man is, in the nature of things, a being of habit, and this he cannot alter; but he can alter his habits. He cannot alter the law of his nature, but he can adapt his nature to the law. No man wishes to alter the law of gravitation, but all men adapt themselves to it; they use it by bending to it, not by defying or ignoring it. Men do not run up against walls or jump over precipices in the hope that the law will alter for them. They walk alongside walls, and keep clear of precipices.

Man can no more get outside the law of habit, than he can get outside the law of gravitation, but he can employ it wisely or unwisely. As scientists and inventors master the physical forces and laws by obeying and using them, so wise men master the spiritual forces and laws in the same way. While the bad man is the whipped slave of habit, the good man is its wise director and master. Not its maker, let me reiterate, nor yet its arbitrary commander, but its self-disciplined user, its master by virtue of knowledge grounded on obedience. He is the bad man whose habits of thought and action are bad. He is the good man whose habits of thought and action are good. The bad man becomes the good man by transforming or transmuting his habits. He does not alter the law; he alters himself; he adapts himself to the law. Instead of submitting to selfish indulgences, he obeys moral principles. He becomes the master of the lower by enlisting in the service of the higher. The law of habit remains the same, but he is changed from bad to good by his readjustment to the law.

Habit is repetition. Man repeats the same thoughts, the same actions, the same experiences over and over again until they are incorporated with his being, until they are built into his character as part of himself. Faculty is fixed habit. Evolution is mental accumulation. Man, today, is the result of millions of repetitious thoughts and acts. He is not readymade, he becomes, and is still becoming. His character is predetermined by his own choice. The thought, the act, which he chooses, that, by habit, he becomes.

Thus each man is an accumulation of thoughts and deeds. The characteristics which he manifests instinctively and without effort are lines of thought and action become, by long repetition, automatic; for it is the nature of habit to become, at last, unconscious, to repeat, as it were, itself without any apparent choice or effort on the part of its possessor; and in due time it takes such complete possession of the individual as to appear to render his will powerless to counteract it. This is the case with all habits, whether good or bad; when bad, the man is spoken of as being the "victim" of a bad habit or a vicious mind; when good, he is referred to as having, by nature, a "good disposition".

All men are, and will continue to be, subject to their own habits, whether they be good or bad—that is, subject to their own reiterated and accumulated thoughts and deeds. Knowing this, the wise man chooses to subject himself to good habits, for such service is joy, bliss, and freedom; while to become subject to bad habits is misery, wretchedness, slavery.

This law of habit is beneficent, for while it enables a man to bind himself to the chains of slavish practices, it enables him to become so fixed in good courses as to do them unconsciously, to instinctively do that which is right, without restraint or exertion, and in perfect happiness and freedom. Observing this automatism in life, men have denied the existence of will or freedom on man's part. They speak of him as being "born" good or bad, and regard him as the helpless instrument of blind forces.

It is true that man is the instrument of mental forces—or, to be more accurate, he is those forces—but they are not blind, and he can direct them, and redirect them into new channels. In a word, he can take himself in hand and reconstruct his habits; for though it is also true that he is born with a given character, that character is the product of numberless lives during which it has been slowly built up by choice and effort, and in this life it will be considerably modified by new experiences.

No matter how apparently helpless a man has become under the tyranny of a bad habit, or a bad characteristic— and both are essentially the same—he can, so long as sanity remains, break away from it and become free, replacing it by its opposite good habit; and when the good possesses him as the bad formerly did, there will be neither wish nor need to break from that, for its dominance will be perennial happiness, and not perpetual misery.

That which a man has formed within himself, he can break up and re-form when he so wishes and wills; and a man does not wish to abandon a bad habit so long as he regards it as pleasurable. It is when it assumes a painful tyranny over him that he begins to look for a way of escape, and finally abandons the bad for something better.

No man is helplessly bound. The very law by which he has become a self-bound slave, will enable him to become a self-emancipated master. To know this, he has but to act upon it—that is, to deliberately and strenuously abandon the old lines of thought and conduct, and diligently fashion new and better lines. That he may not accomplish this in a day, a week, a month, a year, or five years, should not dishearten and dismay him. Time is required for the new repetitions to become established, and the old ones to be broken up; but the law of habit is certain and infallible, and a line of effort patiently pursued and never abandoned, is sure to be crowned with success; for if a bad condition, a mere negation, can become fixed and firm, how much more surely can a good condition, a positive principle, become established and powerful! A man is only powerless to overcome the wrong and unhappy elements in himself so long as he regards himself as powerless. If to the bad habit is added the thought "I cannot" the bad habit will remain. Nothing can be overcome till the thought of powerlessness is uprooted and abolished from the mind. The great stumbling-block is not the habit itself, it is the belief in the impossibility of overcoming it. How can a man overcome a bad habit so long as he is convinced that it is impossible? How can a man be prevented from overcoming it when he knows that he can, and is determined to do it? The dominant thought by which man has enslaved himself is the thought "I cannot overcome my sins." Bring this thought out into the light, in all its nakedness, and it is seen to be a belief in the power of evil, with its other pole, disbelief in the power of good. For a man to say, or believe, that he cannot rise above wrong-thinking and wrong-doing, is to submit to evil, is to abandon and renounce good.

By such thoughts, such beliefs, man binds himself; by their opposite thoughts, opposite beliefs, he sets himself free. A changed attitude of mind changes the character, the habits, the life. Man is his own deliverer. He has brought about his thraldom; he can bring about his emancipation. All through the ages he has looked, and is still looking, for an external deliverer, but he still remains bound. The Great Deliverer is within; He is the Spirit of Truth; and the Spirit of Truth is the Spirit of Good; and he is in the Spirit of Good who dwells habitually in good thoughts and their effects, good actions.

Man is not bound by any power outside his own wrong thoughts, and from these he can set himself free; and foremost, the enslaving thoughts from which he needs to be delivered are—"I cannot rise," "I cannot break away from bad habits," "I cannot alter my nature," "I cannot control and conquer myself", "I CANNOT CEASE FROM SIN." All these "cannots" have no existence in the things to which they submit; they exist only in thought.

Such negations are bad thought-habits which need to be eradicated, and in their place should be planted the positive "I can" which should be tended and developed until it becomes a powerful tree of habit, bearing the good and life-giving fruit of right and happy living.

Habit binds us; habit sets us free. Habit is primarily in thought, secondarily in deed. Turn the thought from bad to good, and the deed will immediately follow. Persist in the bad, and it will bind you tighter and tighter; persist in the good, and it will take you into ever-widening spheres of freedom. He who loves his bondage, let him remain bound. He who thirsts for freedom, let him come and be set free.

19

SOWING AND REAPING

Go into the fields and country lanes in the spring-time, and you will see farmers and gardeners busy sowing seeds in the newly prepared soil. If you were to ask any one of those gardeners or farmers what kind of produce he expected from the seed he was sowing, he would doubtless regard you as foolish, and would tell you that he does not "expect" at all, that it is a matter of common knowledge that his produce will be of the kind which he is sowing, and that he is sowing wheat, or barley, or turnips, as the case may be, in order to reproduce that particular kind.

Every fact and process in Nature contains a moral lesson for the wise man. There is no law in the world of Nature around us which is not to be found operating with the same mathematical certainty in the mind of man and in human life. All the parables of Jesus are illustrative of this truth, and are drawn from the simple facts of Nature. There is a process of seed-sowing in the mind and life a spiritual sowing which leads to a harvest according to the kind of seed sown. Thoughts, words, and acts are seeds sown, and, by the inviolable law of things, they produce after their kind.

The man who thinks hateful thoughts brings hatred upon himself. The man who thinks loving thoughts is loved. The man whose thoughts, words and acts are sincere, is surrounded by sincere friends; the insincere man is surrounded by insincere friends. The man who sows wrong thoughts and deeds, and prays that God will bless him, is in the position of a farmer who, having sown tares, asks God to bring forth for him a harvest of wheat.

> "That which ye sow, ye reap; see yonder fields
> The sesamum was sesamum, the corn
> Was corn; the silence and the darkness knew;
> So is a man's fate born."
> "He cometh reaper of the things he sowed."

He who would be blest, let him scatter blessings. He who would be happy, let him consider the happiness of others.

Then there is another side to this seed sowing. The farmer must scatter all his seed upon the land, and then leave it to the elements. Were he to covetously hoard his seed, he would lose both it and his produce, for his seed would perish. It perishes when he sows it, but in perishing it brings forth a great abundance. So in life, we get by giving; we grow rich by scattering. The man who says he is in possession of knowledge which he cannot give out because the world is incapable of receiving it, either does not possess such knowledge, or, if he does, will soon be deprived of it—if he is not already so deprived. To hoard is to lose; to exclusively retain is to be dispossessed.

Even the man who would increase his material wealth must be willing to part with (invest) what little capital he has, and then wait for the increase. So long as he retains his hold on his precious money, he will not only remain poor, but will be growing poorer everyday. He will, after all, lose the thing he loves, and will lose it without increase. But if he wisely lets it go; if, like the farmer, he scatters his seeds of gold, then he can faithfully wait for, and reasonably expect, the increase.

Men are asking God to give them peace and purity, and righteousness and blessedness, but are not obtaining these things; and why not? Because they are not practising them, not sowing them. I once heard a preacher pray very earnestly for forgiveness, and shortly afterwards, in the course of his sermon, he called upon his congregation to "show no mercy to the enemies of the church." Such self-delusion is pitiful, and men have yet to learn that the way to obtain peace and blessedness is to scatter peaceful and blessed thoughts, words, and deeds.

Men believe that they can sow the seeds of strife, impurity, and unbrotherliness, and then gather in a rich harvest of peace, purity and concord by merely asking for it. What more pathetic sight than to see an irritable and quarrelsome man praying for peace. Men reap that which they sow, and any man can reap all blessedness now and at once, if he will put aside selfishness, and sow broadcast the seeds of kindness, gentleness, and love.

If a man is troubled, perplexed, sorrowful, or unhappy, let him ask:

> "What mental seeds have I been sowing?"
> "What seeds am I sowing?"
> "What have I done for others?"
> "What is my attitude towards others?"
> "What seeds of trouble and sorrow and unhappiness have
> I sown that I should thus reap these bitter weeds?"

Let him seek within and find, and having found, let him abandon all the seeds of self, and sow, henceforth, only the seeds of Truth.

Let him learn of the farmer the simple truths of wisdom.

20

GOOD RESULTS

A considerable portion of the happenings of life comes to us without any direct choosing on our part, and such happenings are generally regarded as having no relation to our will or character, but as appearing fortuitously; as occurring without a cause. Thus one is spoken of as being "lucky," and another "unlucky," the inference being that each has received something which he never earned, never caused. Deeper thought, and a clearer insight into life convinces us, however, that nothing happens without a cause, and that cause and effect are always related in perfect adjustment and harmony. This being so, every happening directly affecting us is intimately related to our own will and character, is, indeed, an effect justly related to a cause having its seat in our consciousness. In a word, involuntary happenings of life are the results of our own thoughts and deeds. This, I admit, is not apparent on the surface; but what fundamental law, even in the physical universe, is so apparent? If thought, investigation, and experiment are necessary to the discovery of the principles which relate one material atom to another, even so are they imperative to the perception and understanding of the mode of action which relate one mental condition to another; and such modes, such laws, are known by the right-doer, by him who has acquired an understanding mind by the practice of true actions.

We reap as we sow. Those things which come to us, though not by our own choosing, are by our causing. The drunkard did not choose the delirium tremens or insanity which overtook him, but he caused it by his own deeds. In this case the law is plain to all minds, but where it is not so plain, it is nonetheless true. Within ourselves is the deep-seated cause of all our sufferings, the spring of all our joys. Alter the inner world of thoughts, and the other world of events will cease to bring you sorrow; make the heart pure, and to you all things will be pure, all occurrences happy and in true order.

> "Within yourselves deliverance must be sought,
> Each man his prison makes.
> Each hath such lordship as the loftiest ones;
> Nay, for with Powers above, around, below,
> As with all flesh and whatsoever lives,
> Act maketh joy or woe."

Our life is good or bad, enslaved or free, according to its causation in our thoughts, for out of these thoughts spring all our deeds, and from these deeds come equitable results. We cannot seize good results violently, like a thief, and claim and enjoy them, but we can bring them to pass by setting in motion the causes within ourselves.

Men strive for money, sigh for happiness, and would gladly possess wisdom, yet fail to secure these things, while they see others to whom these blessings appear to come unbidden. The reason is that they have generated causes which prevent the fulfilment of their wishes and efforts.

Each life is a perfectly woven network of causes and effects, of efforts (or lack of efforts) and results, and good results can only be reached by initiating good efforts, good causes. The doer of true actions, who pursues sound methods, grounded on right principles will not need to strive and struggle for good results; they will be there as the effects of his righteous rule of life. He will reap the fruit of his own actions and the reaping will be in gladness and peace.

This truth of sowing and reaping in the moral sphere is a simple one, yet men are slow to understand and accept it. We have been told by a Wise One that "the children of darkness are wiser in their day than the children of light", and who would expect, in the material world, to reap and eat where he had not sown and planted? Or who would expect to reap wheat in the field where he had sown tares, and would fall to weeping and complaining if he did not? Yet this is just what men do in the spiritual field of mind and deed. They do evil, and expect to get from it good, and when the bitter harvesting comes in all its ripened fullness, they fall into despair, and bemoan the hardness and injustice of their lot, usually attributing it to the evil deeds of others, refusing even to admit the possibility of its cause being hidden in themselves, in their own thoughts and deeds. The children of light—those who are searching for the fundamental principles of right living, with a view to making themselves into wise and happy beings—must train themselves to observe this law of cause and effect in thought, word and deed, as implicitly and obediently as the gardener obeys the law of sowing and reaping. He does not even question the law; he recognises and obeys it. When the wisdom which he instinctively practices in his garden, is practiced by men in the garden of their minds— when the law of the sowing of deeds is so fully recognised that it can no longer be doubted or questioned—then it will be just as faithfully followed by the sowing of those actions which will bring about a reaping of happiness and well-being for all. As the children of matter obey the laws of matter, so let the children of spirit obey the laws of spirit, for the law of matter and the law of spirit are one; they are but two aspects of one thing; the out-working of one principle in opposite directions.

If we observe right principles, or causes, wrong effects cannot possibly accrue. If we pursue sound methods, no shoddy thread can find its way into the web of our life, no rotten brick enter into the building of our character to render it insecure; and if we do true actions, what but good results can come to pass; for to say that good causes can produce bad effects is to say that nettles can be reaped from a sowing of corn.

He who orders his life along the moral lines thus briefly enunciated, will attain to such a state of insight and equilibrium as to render him permanently happy and perennially glad; all his efforts will be seasonally planted; all the issues of his life will be good, and though he may not become a millionaire as indeed he will have no desire to become such—he will acquire the gift of peace, and true success will wait upon him as its commanding master.

21

THE LESSON OF EVIL

Unrest and pain and sorrow are the shadows of life. There is no heart in all the world that has not felt the sting of pain, no mind has not been tossed upon the dark waters of trouble, no eye that has not wept the hot blinding tears of unspeakable anguish.

There is no household where the Great Destroyers, disease and death, have not entered, severing heart from heart, and casting over all the dark pall of sorrow. In the strong, and apparently indestructible meshes of evil all are more or less fast caught, and pain, unhappiness, and misfortune wait upon mankind.

With the object of escaping, or in some way mitigating this overshadowing gloom, men and women rush blindly into innumerable devices, pathways by which they fondly hope to enter into a happiness which will not pass away.

Such are the drunkard and the harlot, who revel in sensual excitements; such is the exclusive aesthete, who shuts himself out from the sorrows of the world, and surrounds himself with enervating luxuries; such is he who thirsts for wealth or fame, and subordinates all things to the achievement of that object; and such are they who seek consolation in the performance of religious rites.

And to all the happiness sought seems to come, and the soul, for a time, is lulled into a sweet security, and an intoxicating forgetfulness of the existence of evil; but the day of disease comes at last, or some great sorrow, temptation, or misfortune breaks suddenly in on the unfortified soul, and the fabric of its fancied happiness is torn to shreds.

So over the head of every personal joy hangs the Damocletian sword of pain, ready, at any moment, to fall and crush the soul of him who is unprotected by knowledge.

The child cries to be a man or woman; the man and woman sigh for the lost felicity of childhood. The poor man chafes under the chains of poverty by which he is bound, and the rich man often lives in fear of poverty, or scours the world in search of an elusive shadow he calls happiness.

Sometimes the soul feels that it has found a secure peace and happiness in adopting a certain religion, in embracing an intellectual philosophy, or in building up an intellectual or artistic ideal; but some overpowering temptation proves the religion to be inadequate or insufficient; the theoretical philosophy is found to be a useless prop; or in a moment, the idealistic statue upon which the devotee has for years been laboring, is shattered into fragments at his feet.

Is there, then, no way of escape from pain and sorrow? Are there no means by which bonds of evil may be broken? Is permanent happiness, secure prosperity, and abiding peace a foolish dream?

No, there is a way, and I speak it with gladness, by which evil can be slain for ever; there is a process by which disease, poverty, or any adverse condition or circumstance can be put on one side never to return; there is a method by which a permanent prosperity can be secured, free from all fear of the return of adversity, and there is a practice by which unbroken and unending peace and bliss can be partaken of and realized.

And the beginning of the way which leads to this glorious realization is the acquirement of a right understanding of the nature of evil.

It is not sufficient to deny or ignore evil; it must be understood. It is not enough to pray to God to remove the evil; you must find out why it is there, and what lesson it has for you.

It is of no avail to fret and fume and chafe at the chains which bind you; you must know why and how you are bound. Therefore, reader, you must get outside yourself, and must begin to examine and understand yourself.

You must cease to be a disobedient child in the school of experience and must begin to learn, with humility and patience, the lessons that are set for your edification and ultimate perfection; for evil, when rightly understood, is found to be, not an unlimited power or principle in the universe, but a passing phase of human experience, and it therefore becomes a teacher to those who are willing to learn.

Evil is not an abstract some thing outside yourself; it is an experience in your own heart, and by patiently examining and rectifying your heart you will be gradually led into the discovery of the origin and nature of evil, which will necessarily be followed by its complete eradication.

All evil is corrective and remedial, and is therefore not permanent. It is rooted in ignorance, ignorance of the true nature and relation of things, and so long as we remain in that state of ignorance, we remain subject to evil.

There is no evil in the universe which is not the result of ignorance, and which would not, if we were ready and willing to learn its lesson, lead us to higher wisdom, and then vanish away. But men remain in evil, and it does not pass away because men are not willing or prepared to learn the lesson which it came to teach them.

I knew a child who, every night when its mother took it to bed, cried to be allowed to play with the candle; and one night, when the mother was off guard for a moment, the child took hold of the candle; the inevitable result followed, and the child never wished to play with the candle again.

By its one foolish act it learned, and learned perfectly the lesson of obedience, and entered into the knowledge that fire burns. And, this incident is a complete illustration of the nature, meaning, and ultimate result of all sin and evil.

As the child suffered through its own ignorance of the real nature of fire, so older children suffer through their ignorance of the real nature of the things which they weep for and strive after, and which harm them when they are secured; the only difference being that in the latter case the ignorance and evil are more deeply rooted and obscure.

Evil has always been symbolized by darkness, and Good by light, and hidden within the symbol is contained the perfect interpretation, the reality; for, just as light always floods the universe, and darkness is only a mere speck or shadow cast by a small body intercepting a few rays of the illimitable light, so the Light of the Supreme Good is the positive and life-giving power which floods the universe, and evil the insignificant shadow cast by the self that intercepts and shuts off the illuminating rays which strive for entrance.

When night folds the world in its black impenetrable mantle, no matter how dense the darkness, it covers but the small space of half our little planet, while the whole universe is ablaze with living light, and every soul knows that it will awake in the light in the morning.

Know, then, that when the dark night of sorrow, pain, or misfortune settles down upon your soul, and you stumble along with weary and uncertain steps, that you are merely intercepting your own personal desires between yourself and the boundless light of joy and bliss, and the dark shadow that covers you is cast by none and nothing but yourself.

And just as the darkness without is but a negative shadow, an unreality which comes from nowhere, goes to nowhere, and has no abiding dwelling place, so the darkness within is equally a negative shadow passing over the evolving and Lightborn soul.

"But," I fancy I hear someone say, "why pass through the darkness of evil at all?" Because, by ignorance, you have chosen to do so, and because, by doing so, you may understand both good and evil, and may the more appreciate the light by having passed through the darkness.

As evil is the direct outcome of ignorance, so, when the lessons of evil are fully learned, ignorance passes away, and wisdom takes its place. But as a disobedient child refuses to learn its lessons at school, so it is possible to refuse to learn the lessons of experience, and thus to remain in continual darkness, and to suffer continually recurring punishments in the form of disease, disappointment, and sorrow.

He, therefore, who would shake himself free of the evil which encompasses him, must be willing and ready to learn, and must be prepared to undergo that disciplinary process without which no grain of wisdom or abiding happiness and peace can be secured.

A man may shut himself up in a dark room, and deny that the light exists, but it is everywhere without, and darkness exists only in his own little room.

So you may shut out the light of Truth, or you may begin to pull down the walls of prejudice, self-seeking and error which you have built around yourself, and so let in the glorious and omnipresent Light.

By earnest self-examination strive to realize, and not merely hold as a theory, that evil is a passing phase, a self-created shadow; that all your pains, sorrows and misfortunes have come to you by a process of undeviating and absolutely perfect law;

have come to you because you deserve and require them, and that by first enduring, and then understanding them, you may be made stronger, wiser, nobler.

When you have fully entered into this realization, you will be in a position to mould your own circumstances, to transmute all evil into good and to weave, with a master hand, the fabric of your destiny.

What of the night, O Watchman! see'st thou yet
The glimmering dawn upon the mountain heights,
The golden Herald of the Light of lights,
Are his fair feet upon the hilltops set?

Cometh he yet to chase away the gloom,
And with it all the demons of the Night?
Strike yet his darting rays upon thy sight?
Hear'st thou his voice, the sound of error's doom?

The Morning cometh, lover of the Light;
Even now He gilds with gold the mountain's brow,
Dimly I see the path whereon even now
His shining feet are set toward the Night.

Darkness shall pass away, and all the things
That love the darkness, and that hate the Light
Shall disappear for ever with the Night:
Rejoice! for thus the speeding Herald sings.

22

THE WAY OUT OF
UNDESIRABLE CONDITIONS

Having seen and realized that evil is but a passing shadow thrown, by the intercepting self, across the transcendent Form of the Eternal Good, and that the world is a mirror in which each sees a reflection of himself, we now ascend, by firm and easy steps, to that plane of perception whereon is seen and realized the Vision of the Law.

With this realization comes the knowledge that everything is included in a ceaseless interaction of cause and effect, and that nothing can possibly be divorced from law.

From the most trivial thought, word, or act of man, up to the groupings of the celestial bodies, law reigns supreme. No arbitrary condition can, even for one moment, exist, for such a condition would be a denial and an annihilation of law.

Every condition of life is, therefore, bound up in an orderly and harmonious sequence, and the secret and cause of every condition is contained within itself, The law, "Whatsoever a man sows that shall he also reap," is inscribed in flaming letters upon the portal of Eternity, and none can deny it, none can cheat it, none can escape it.

He who puts his hand in the fire must suffer the burning until such time as it has worked itself out, and neither curses nor prayers can avail to alter it.

And precisely the same law governs the realm of mind. Hatred, anger, jealousy, envy, lust, covetousness, all these are fires which bum, and whoever even so much as touches them must suffer the torments of burning.

All these conditions of mind are rightly called "evil," for they are the efforts of the soul to subvert, in its ignorance, the law, an they, therefore, lead to chaos and confusion within, and are sooner or later actualized in the outward circumstances as disease, failure, and misfortune, coupled with grief, pain, and despair.

Whereas love, gentleness, good-will, purity, are cooling airs which breathe peace upon the soul that woes them, and, being in harmony with the Eternal Law, they become actualized in the form of health, peaceful surroundings, and undeviating success and good fortune.

A thorough understanding of this Great Law which permeates the universe leads to the acquirement of that state of mind known as obedience.

To know that justice, harmony, and love are supreme in the universe is likewise to know that all adverse and painful conditions are the result of our own disobedience to that Law.

Such knowledge leads to strength and power, and it is upon such knowledge alone that a true life and an enduring success and happiness can be built.

To be patient under all circumstances, and to accept all conditions as necessary factors in your training, is to rise superior to all painful conditions, and to overcome them with an overcoming which is sure, and which leaves no fear of their return, for by the power of obedience to law they are utterly slain.

Such an obedient one is working in harmony with the law, has in fact, identified himself with the law, and whatsoever he conquers he conquers for ever, whatsoever he builds can never be destroyed.

The cause of all power, as of all weakness, is within; the secret of all happiness as of all misery is likewise within.

There is no progress apart from unfoldment within, and no sure foothold of prosperity or peace except by orderly advancement in knowledge.

You say you are chained by circumstances; you cry out for better opportunities, for a wider scope, for improved physical conditions, and perhaps you inwardly curse the fate that binds you hand and foot.

It is for you that I write; it is to you that I speak. Listen, and let my words burn themselves into your heart, for that which I say to you is truth:

You may bring about that improved condition in your outward life which you desire, if you will unswervingly resolve to improve your inner life.

I know this pathway looks barren at its commencement (truth always does, it is only error and delusion which are at first inviting and fascinating,) but if you undertake to walk it; if you perseveringly discipline your mind, eradicating your weaknesses, and allowing your soul-forces and spiritual powers to unfold themselves, you will be astonished at the magical changes which will be brought about in your outward life.

As you proceed, golden opportunities will be strewn across your path, and the power and judgment to properly utilize them will spring up within you. Genial friends will come unbidden to you; sympathetic souls will be drawn to you as the needle is to the magnet; and books and all outward aids that you require will come to you unsought.

Perhaps the chains of poverty hang heavily upon you, and you are friendless and alone, and you long with an intense longing that your load may be lightened; but the load continues, and you seem to be enveloped in an ever-increasing darkness.

Perhaps you complain, you bewail your lot; you blame your birth, your parents, your employer, or the unjust Powers who have bestowed upon you so undeservedly poverty and hardship, and upon another affluence and ease.

Cease your complaining and fretting; none of these things which you blame are the cause of your poverty; the cause is within yourself, and where the cause is, there is the remedy.

The very fact that you are a complainer, shows that you deserve your lot; shows that you lack that faith which is the ground of all effort and progress.

There is no room for a complainer in a universe of law, and worry is soul-suicide. By your very attitude of mind you are strengthening the chains which bind you, and are drawing about you the darkness by which you are enveloped, Alter your outlook upon life, and your outward life will alter.

Build yourself up in the faith and knowledge, and make yourself worthy of better surroundings and wider opportunities. Be sure, first of all, that you are making the best of what you have.

Do not delude yourself into supposing that you can step into greater advantages whilst overlooking smaller ones, for if you could, the advantage would be impermanent and you would quickly fall back again in order to learn the lesson which you had neglected.

As the child at school must master one standard before passing onto the next, so, before you can have that greater good which you so desire, must you faithfully employ that which you already possess.

The parable of the talents is a beautiful story illustrative of this truth, for does it not plainly show that if we misuse, neglect, or degrade that which we possess, be it ever so mean and insignificant, even that little will be taken from us, for, by our conduct we show that we are unworthy of it.

Perhaps you are living in a small cottage, and are surrounded by unhealthy and vicious influences.

You desire a larger and more sanitary residence. Then you must fit yourself for such a residence by first of all making your cottage as far as possible a little paradise. Keep it spotlessly clean. Make it look as pretty and sweet as your limited means will allow. Cook your plain food with all care, and arrange your humble table as tastefully as you possibly can.

Even poverty and lack of time and leisure are not the evils that you imagine they are, and if they hinder you in your progress, it is because you have clothed them in your own weaknesses, and the evil that you see in them is really in yourself. Endeavor to fully and completely realize that in so far as you shape and mould your mind, you are the maker of your destiny, and as, by the transmuting power of self-discipline you realize this more and more, you will come to see that these so-called evils may be converted into blessings.

You will then utilize your poverty for the cultivation of patience, hope and courage; and your lack of time in the gaining of promptness of action and decision of mind, by seizing the precious moments as they present themselves for your acceptance.

As in the rankest soil the most beautiful flowers are grown, so in the dark soil of poverty the choicest flowers of humanity have developed and bloomed.

Where there are difficulties to cope with, and unsatisfactory conditions to overcome, there virtue most flourishes and manifests its glory.

It may be that you are in the employ of a tyrannous master or mistress, and you feel that you are harshly treated. Look upon this also as necessary to your training. Return your employer's unkindness with gentleness and forgiveness.

Practice unceasingly patience and self-control. Turn the disadvantage to account by utilizing it for the gaining of mental and spiritual strength, and by your silent example and influence you will thus be teaching your employer, will be helping him to grow ashamed of his conduct, and will, at the same time, be lifting yourself up to that height of spiritual attainment by which you will be enabled to step into new and more congenial surroundings at the time when they are presented to you.

Do not complain that you are a slave, but lift yourself up, by noble conduct, above the plane of slavery. Before complaining that you are a slave to another, be sure that you are not a slave to self.

Look within; look searchingly, and have no mercy upon yourself. You will find there, perchance, slavish thoughts, slavish desires, and in your daily life and conduct slavish habits.

Conquer these; cease to be a slave to self, and no man will have the power to enslave you. As you overcome self, you will overcome all adverse conditions, and every difficulty will fall before you.

Do not complain that you are oppressed by the rich. Are you sure that if you gained riches you would not be an oppressor yourself?

Remember that there is the Eternal Law which is absolutely just, and that he who oppresses today must himself be oppressed tomorrow; and from this there is no way of escape.

And perhaps you, yesterday (in some former existence) were rich and an oppressor, and that you are now merely paying off the debt which you owe to the Great Law. Practice, therefore, fortitude and faith.

Dwell constantly in mind upon the Eternal justice, the

Eternal Good. Endeavor to lift yourself above the personal and the transitory into the impersonal and permanent.

Shake off the delusion that you are being injured or oppressed by another, and try to realize, by a profounder comprehension of your inner life, and the laws which govern that life, that you are only really injured by what is within you. There is no practice more degrading, debasing, and soul-destroying than that of self-pity.

Cast it out from you. While such a canker is feeding upon your heart you can never expect to grow into a fuller life.

Cease from the condemnation of others, and begin to condemn yourself. Condone none of your acts, desires or thoughts that will not bear comparison with spotless purity, or endure the light of sinless good.

By so doing you will be building your house upon the rock of the Eternal, and all that is required for your happiness and well-being will come to you in its own time.

There is positively no way of permanently rising above poverty, or any undesirable condition, except by eradicating those selfish and negative conditions within, of which these are the reflection, and by virtue of which they continue.

The way to true riches is to enrich the soul by the acquisition of virtue. Outside of real heart-virtue there is neither prosperity nor power, but only the appearances of these. I am aware that men make money who have acquired no measure of virtue, and have little desire to do so; but such money does not constitute true riches, and its possession is transitory and feverish.

Here is David's testimony: "For I was envious at the foolish when I saw the prosperity of the wicked...... Their eyes stand out with fatness; they have more than heart could wish. Verily I have cleansed my heart in vain, and washed my hands in innocence... When I thought to know this it was too painful for me; until I went into the sanctuary of God, then understood I their end."

The prosperity of the wicked was a great trial to David until he went into the sanctuary of God, and then he knew their end.

You likewise may go into that sanctuary. It is within you. It is that state of consciousness which remains when all that is sordid, and personal, and impermanent is risen above, and universal and eternal principles are realized.

That is the God state of consciousness; it is the sanctuary of the Most High. When by long strife and self-discipline, you have succeeded in entering the door of that holy Temple, you will perceive, with unobstructed vision, the end and fruit of all human thought and endeavor, both good and evil.

You will then no longer relax your faith when you see the immoral man accumulating outward riches, for you will know, that he must come again to poverty and degradation.

The rich man who is barren of virtue is, in reality, poor, and as surely, as the waters of the river are drifting to the ocean, so surely is he, in the midst of all his riches, drifting towards poverty and misfortune; and though he die rich, yet must he return to reap the bitter fruit of all of his immorality.

And though he become rich many times, yet as many times must he be thrown back into poverty, until, by long experience and suffering he conquers the poverty within.

But the man who is outwardly poor, yet rich in virtue, is truly rich, and, in the midst of all his poverty he is surely traveling towards prosperity; and abounding joy and bliss await his coming. If you would become truly and permanently prosperous, you must first become virtuous.

It is therefore unwise to aim directly at prosperity, to make it the one object of life, to reach out greedily for it, To do this is to ultimately defeat yourself.

But rather aim at self-perfection, make useful and unselfish service the object of your life, and ever reach out hands of faith towards the supreme and unalterable Good.

You say you desire wealth, not for your own sake, but in order to do good with it, and to bless others. If this is your real motive in desiring wealth, then wealth will come to you; for you are strong and unselfish indeed if, in the midst of riches, you are willing to look upon yourself as steward and not as owner.

But examine well your motive, for in the majority of instances where money is desired for the admitted object of blessing others, the real underlying motive is a love of popularity, and a desire to pose as a philanthropist or reformer.

If you are not doing good with what little you have, depend upon it the more money you got the more selfish you would become, and all the good you appeared to do with your money, if you attempted to do any, would be so much insinuating self-laudation.

If your real desire is to do good, there is no need to wait for money before you do it; you can do it now, this very moment, and just where you are. If you are really so unselfish as you believe yourself to be, you will show it by sacrificing yourself for others now.

No matter how poor you are, there is room for self-sacrifice, for did not the widow put her all into the treasury?

The heart that truly desires to do good does not wait for money before doing it, but comes to the altar of sacrifice and, leaving there the unworthy elements of self, goes out and breathes upon neighbor and stranger, friend and enemy alike the breath of blessedness.

As the effect is related to the cause, so is prosperity and power related to the inward good and poverty and weakness to the inward evil.

Money does not constitute true wealth, nor position, nor power, and to rely upon it alone is to stand upon a slippery place.

Your true wealth is your stock of virtue, and your true power the uses to which you put it. Rectify your heart, and you will rectify your life. Lust, hatred, anger, vanity, pride, covetousness, self-indulgence, self-seeking, obstinacy,- all these are poverty and weakness; whereas love, purity, gentleness, meekness, compassion, generosity, self-forgetfulness, and self-renunciation,- all these are wealth and power.

As the elements of poverty and weakness are overcome, an irresistible and allconquering power is evolved from within, and he who succeeds in establishing himself in the highest virtue, brings the whole world to his feet.

But the rich, as well as the poor, have their undesirable conditions, and are frequently farther removed from happiness than the poor. And here we see how happiness depends, not upon outward aids or possessions, but upon the inward life.

Perhaps you are an employer, and you have endless trouble with those whom you employ, and when you do get good and faithful servants they quickly leave you. As a result you are beginning to lose, or have completely lost, your faith in human nature.

You try to remedy matters by giving better wages, and by allowing certain liberties, yet matters remain unaltered. Let me advise you.

The secret of all your trouble is not in your servants, it is in yourself; and if you look within, with a humble and sincere desire to discover and eradicate your error, you will, sooner or later, find the origin of all your unhappiness.

It may be some selfish desire, or lurking suspicion, or unkind attitude of mind which sends out its poison upon those about you, and reacts upon yourself, even though you may not show it in your manner or speech.

Think of your servants with kindness, consider of them that extremity of service which you yourself would not care to perform were you in their place.

Rare and beautiful is that humility of soul by which a servant entirely forgets himself in his master's good; but far rarer, and beautiful with a divine beauty, is that nobility of soul by which a man, forgetting his own happiness, seeks the happiness of those who are under his authority, and who depend upon him for their bodily sustenance.

And such a man's happiness is increased tenfold, nor does he need to complain of those whom he employs. Said a well known and extensive employer of labor, who never needs to dismiss an employee: "I have always had the happiest relations with my workpeople.

If you ask me how it is to be accounted for, I can only say that it has been my aim from the first to do to them as I would wish to be done by." Herein lies the secret by which all desirable conditions are secured, and all that are undesirable are overcome.

Do you say that you are lonely and unloved, and have "not a friend in the world"? Then, I pray you, for the sake of your own happiness, blame nobody but yourself.

Be friendly towards others, and friends will soon flock round you. Make yourself pure and lovable, and you will be loved by all.

Come, then, out of your poverty; come out of your pain; come out of your troubles, and sighings, and complainings, and heartaches, and loneliness by coming out of yourself.

Let the old tattered garment of your petty selfishness fall from you, and put on the new garment of universal Love. You will then realize the inward heaven, and it will be reflected in all your outward life.

He who sets his foot firmly upon the path of self-conquest, who walks, aided by the staff of Faith, the highway of self-sacrifice, will assuredly achieve the highest prosperity, and will reap abounding and enduring joy and bliss.

> To them that seek the highest good
> All things subserve the wisest ends;
> Nought comes as ill, and wisdom lends
> Wings to all shapes of evil brood.
>
> The dark'ning sorrow veils a Star
> That waits to shine with gladsome light;
> Hell waits on heaven; and after night
> Comes golden glory from afar.
>
> Defeats are steps by which we climb
> With purer aim to nobler ends;
> Loss leads to gain, and joy attends
> True footsteps up the hills of time.
>
> Pain leads to paths of holy bliss,
> To thoughts and words and deeds divine-,
> And clouds that gloom and rays that shine,
> Along life's upward highway kiss.
>
> Misfortune does but cloud the way
> Whose end and summit in the sky
> Of bright success, sunkiss'd and high,
> Awaits our seeking and our stay.
>
> The heavy pall of doubts and fears
> That clouds the Valley of our hopes,
> The shades with which the spirit copes,
> The bitter harvesting of tears,

The heartaches, miseries, and griefs,
The bruisings born of broken ties,
All these are steps by which we rise
To living ways of sound beliefs.

Love, pitying, watchful, runs to meet
The Pilgrim from the Land of Fate;
All glory and all good await
The coming of obedient feet.

23

CONQUEST: NOT RESIGNATION

He who has undertaken the sublime task of overcoming himself, does not resign himself to anything that is evil; he subjects himself only to that which is good. Resignation to evil is the lowest weakness; obedience to good is the highest power. To resign oneself to sin and sorrow, to ignorance and suffering, is to say in effect, "I give up; I am defeated; life is evil, and I submit." Such resignation to evil is the reverse of religion. It is a direct denial of good; it elevates evil to the position of supreme power in the universe. Such submission to evil shows itself in a selfish and sorrowful life; a life alike devoid of strength against temptation, and of that joy and calm which are the manifestation of a mind that is dominated by good.

Man is not framed for perpetual resignation and sorrow, but for final victory and joy. All the spiritual laws of the universe are with the good man, for good preserves and shields. There are no laws of evil. Its nature is destruction and desolation.

The doctrine herein set forth by the author is the doctrine of conquest over evil; the annihilation of sin; and necessarily the permanent establishment of man in the knowledge of good, and in the enjoyment of perpetual peace. This is the teaching of the Masters of religion in all ages. Howsoever it may have been disguised and distorted by the unenlightened, if is the doctrine of all the perfect ones that were, and will be the doctrine of all the perfect ones that are to come. It is the doctrine of Truth.

And the conquest is not of an evil without; not of evil men, or evil spirits, or evil things; but of the evil within; of evil thoughts, evil desires, evil deeds; for when every man has destroyed the evil within his own heart, to where in the whole vast universe will any one be able to point, and say, "There is evil?" In that great day when all men have become good within, all traces of evil will have vanished from the earth; sin and sorrow will be unknown; and there will be universal joy for evermore.

24

THE SILENT POWER OF THOUGHT: CONTROLLING AND DIRECTING ONE'S FORCES

The most powerful forces in the universe are the silent forces; and in accordance with the intensity of its power does a force become beneficent when rightly directed, and destructive when wrongly employed.

This is a common knowledge in regard to the mechanical forces, such as steam, electricity, etc., but few have yet learned to apply this knowledge to the realm of mind, where the thought-forces (most powerful of all) are continually being generated and sent forth as currents of salvation or destruction.

At this stage of his evolution, man has entered into the possession of these forces, and the whole trend of his present advancement is their complete subjugation. All the wisdom possible to man on this material earth is to be found only in complete self-mastery, and the command, "Love your enemies," resolves itself into an exhortation to enter here and now, into the possession of that sublime wisdom by taking hold of, mastering and transmuting, those mind forces to which man is now slavishly subject, and by which he is helplessly borne, like a straw on the stream, upon the currents of selfishness.

The Hebrew prophets, with their perfect knowledge of the Supreme Law, always related outward events to inward thought, and associated national disaster or success with the thoughts and desires that dominated the nation at the time.

The knowledge of the causal power of thought is the basis of all their prophecies, as it is the basis of all real wisdom and power. National events are simply the working out of the psychic forces of the nation.

Wars, plagues, and famines are the meeting and clashing of wrongly-directed thought-forces, the culminating points at which destruction steps in as the agent of the Law.

It is foolish to ascribe war to the influence of one man, or to one body of men. It is the crowning horror of national selfishness. It is the silent and conquering thought-forces which bring all things into manifestation.

The universe grew out of thought. Matter in its last analysis is found to be merely objectivized thought. All men's accomplishments were first wrought out in thought, and then objectivized.

The author, the inventor, the architect, first builds up his work in thought, and having perfected it in all its parts as a complete and harmonious whole upon the thought-plane. he then commences to materialize it, to bring it down to the material or sense-plane.

When the thought-forces are directed in harmony with the over-ruling Law, they are up-building and preservative, but when subverted they become disintegrating and self-destructive.

To adjust all your thoughts to a perfect and unswerving faith in the omnipotence and supremacy of Good, is to co-operate with that Good, and to realize within yourself the solution and destruction of all evil. Believe and ye shall live.

And here we have the true meaning of salvation; salvation from the darkness and negation of evil, by entering into, and realizing the living light of the Eternal Good.

Where there is fear, worry, anxiety, doubt, trouble, chagrin, or disappointment, there is ignorance and lack of faith.

All these conditions of mind are the direct outcome of selfishness, and are based upon an inherent belief in the power and supremacy of evil; they therefore constitute practical atheism; and to live in, and become subject to, these negative and soul-destroying conditions of mind is the only real atheism.

It is salvation from such conditions that the race needs, and let no man boast of salvation whilst he is their helpless and obedient slave.

To fear or to worry is as sinful as to curse, for how can one fear or worry if he intrinsically believes in the Eternal justice, the Omnipotent Good, the Boundless Love? To fear, to worry, to doubt, is to deny, to dis-believe.

It is from such states of mind that all weakness and failure proceed, for they represent the annulling and disintegrating of the positive thought-forces which would otherwise speed to their object with power, and bring about their own beneficent results.

To overcome these negative conditions is to enter into a life of power, is to cease to be a slave, and to become a master, and there is only one way by which they can be overcome, and that is by steady and persistent growth in inward knowledge.

To mentally deny evil is not sufficient; it must, by daily practice, be risen above and understood. To mentally affirm the good is inadequate; it must, by unswerving endeavor, be entered into and comprehended.

The intelligent practice of self-control, quickly leads to a knowledge of one's interior thought-forces, and, later on, to the acquisition of that power by which they are rightly employed and directed.

In the measure that you master self, that you control your

mental forces instead of being controlled by them, in just such measure will you master affairs and outward circumstances.

Show me a man under whose touch everything crumbles away, and who cannot retain success even when it is placed in his hands, and I will show you a man who dwells continually in those conditions of mind which are the very negation of power.

To be for ever wallowing in the bogs of doubt, to be drawn continually into the quicksands of fear, or blown ceaselessly about by the winds of anxiety, is to be a slave, and to live the life of a slave, even though success and influence be for ever knocking at your door seeking for admittance.

Such a man, being without faith and without self-government, is incapable of the right government of his affairs, and is a slave to circumstances; in reality a slave to himself. Such are taught by affliction, and ultimately pass from weakness to strength by the stress of bitter experience. Faith and purpose constitute the motive-power of life.

There is nothing that a strong faith and an unflinching purpose may not accomplish. By the daily exercise of silent faith, the thought-forces are gathered together, and by the daily strengthening of silent purpose, those forces are directed toward the object of accomplishment.

Whatever your position in life may be, before you can hope to enter into any measure of success, usefulness, and power, you must learn how to focus your thought-forces by cultivating calmness and repose. It may be that you are a business man, and you are suddenly confronted with some overwhelming difficulty or probable disaster. You grow fearful and anxious, and are at your wit's end.

To persist in such a state of mind would be fatal, for when anxiety steps in, correct judgment passes out. Now if you will take advantage of a quiet hour or two in the early morning or at night, and go away to some solitary spot, or to some room in your house where you know you will be absolutely free from intrusion, and, having seated yourself in an easy attitude, you forcibly direct your mind right away from the object of anxiety by dwelling upon something in your life that is pleasing and blissgiving, a calm, reposeful strength will gradually steal into your mind, and your anxiety will pass away.

Upon the instant that you find your mind reverting to the lower plane of worry bring it back again, and re-establish it on the plane of peace and strength.

When this is fully accomplished, you may then concentrate your whole mind upon the solution of your difficulty, and what was intricate and insurmountable to you in your hour of anxiety will be made plain and easy, and you will see, with that clear vision and perfect judgment which belong only to a calm and untroubled mind, the right course to pursue and the proper end to be brought about.

It may be that you will have to try day after day before you will be able to perfectly calm your mind, but if you persevere you will certainly accomplish it. And the course which is presented to you in that hour of calmness must be carried out.

Every thought you think is a force sent out, and in accordance with its nature and intensity will it go out to seek a lodgment in minds receptive to it, and will react upon yourself for good or evil. There is ceaseless reciprocity between mind and mind, and a continual interchange of thought-forces.

Selfish and disturbing thoughts are so many malignant and destructive forces, messengers of evil, sent out to stimulate and augment the evil in other minds, which in turn send them back upon you with added power.

While thoughts that are calm, pure, and unselfish are so many angelic messengers sent out into the world with health, healing, and blessedness upon their wings, counteracting the evil forces; pouring the oil of joy upon the troubled waters of anxiety and sorrow, and restoring to broken hearts their heritage of immortality.

Think good thoughts, and they will quickly become actualized in your outward life in the form of good conditions. Control your soul-forces, and you will be able to shape your outward life as you will.

The difference between a savior and a sinner is this, that the one has a perfect control of all the forces within him; the other is dominated and controlled by them.

There is absolutely no other way to true power and abiding peace, but by self-control, self-government, self-purification. To be at the mercy of your disposition is to be impotent, unhappy, and of little real use in the world.

The conquest of your petty likes and dislikes, your capricious loves and hates, your fits of anger, suspicion, jealousy, and all the changing moods to which you are more or less helplessly subject, this is the task you have before you if you would weave into the web of life the golden threads of happiness and prosperity.

In so far as you are enslaved by the changing moods within you, will you need to depend upon others and upon outward aids as you walk through life.

If you would walk firmly and securely, and would accomplish any achievement, you must learn to rise above and control all such disturbing and retarding vibrations.

You must daily practice the habit of putting your mind at rest, "going into the silence," as it is commonly called. This is a method of replacing a troubled thought with one of peace, a thought of weakness with one of strength.

Until you succeed in doing this you cannot hope to direct

your mental forces upon the problems and pursuits of life with any appreciable measure of success. It is a process of diverting one's scattered forces into one powerful channel.

Just as a useless marsh may be converted into a field of golden corn or a fruitful garden by draining and directing the scattered and harmful streams into one wellcut channel, so, he who acquires calmness, and subdues and directs the thoughtcurrents within himself, saves his soul, and fructifies his heart and life.

As you succeed in gaining mastery over your impulses and thoughts you will begin to feel, growing up within you, a new and silent power, and a settled feeling of composure and strength will remain with you.

Your latent powers will begin to unfold themselves, and whereas formerly your efforts were weak and ineffectual, you will now be able to work with that calm confidence which commands success.

And along with this new power and strength, there will be awakened within you that interior Illumination known as "intuition," and you will walk no longer in darkness and speculation, but in light and certainty.

With the development of this soul-vision, judgment and mental penetration will be incalculably increased, and there will evolve within you that prophetic vision by the aid of which you will be able to sense coming events, and to forecast, with remarkable accuracy, the result of your efforts.

And in just the measure that you alter from within will your outlook upon life alter; and as you alter your mental attitude towards others they will alter in their attitude and conduct toward you.

As you rise above the lower, debilitating, and destructive thought-forces, you will come in contact with the positive, strengthening, and up-building currents generated by strong, pure, and noble minds, your happiness will be immeasurably intensified, and you will begin to realize the joy, strength, and power, which are born only of self-mastery.

And this joy, strength, and power will be continually radiating from you, and without any effort on your part, nay, though you are utterly unconscious of it, strong people will be drawn toward you, influence will be put into your hands, and in accordance with your altered thought-world will outward events shape themselves.

"A man's foes are they of his own household," and he who would be useful, strong, and happy, must cease to be a passive receptacle for the negative, beggardly, and impure streams of thought; and as a wise householder commands his servants and invites his guests, so must he learn to command his desires, and to say, with authority, what thoughts he shall admit into the mansion of his soul.

Even a very partial success in self-mastery adds greatly to one's power, and he who succeeds in perfecting this divine accomplishment, enters into possession of undreamed-of wisdom and inward strength and peace, and realizes that all the forces of the universe aid and protect his footsteps who is master of his soul.

> Would you scale the highest heaven,
> Would you pierce the lowest hell,
> Live in dreams of constant beauty,
> Or in basest thinkings dwell.
>
> For your thoughts are heaven above you,
> And your thoughts are hell below,
> Bliss is not, except in thinking,
> Torment nought but thought can know.

Worlds would vanish but for thinking;
Glory is not but in dreams;
And the Drama of the ages
From the Thought Eternal streams.

Dignity and shame and sorrow,
Pain and anguish, love and hate
Are but maskings of the mighty
Pulsing Thought that governs Fate.

As the colors of the rainbow
Makes the one uncolored beam,
So the universal changes
Make the One Eternal Dream.

And the Dream is all within you,
And the Dreamer waiteth long
For the Morning to awake him
To the living thought and strong.

That shall make the ideal real,
Make to vanish dreams of hell
In the highest, holiest heaven
Where the pure and perfect dwell.

Evil is the thought that thinks it;
Good, the thought that makes it so
Light and darkness, sin and pureness
Likewise out of thinking grow.

Dwell in thought upon the Grandest,
And the Grandest you shall see ;
Fix your mind upon the Highest,
And the Highest you shall be.

25

PRACTICE OF MEDITATION

When aspiration is united to concentration, the result is meditation. When a man intensely desires to reach and realize a higher, purer, and more radiant life than the merely worldly and pleasure loving life, he engages in aspiration; and when he earnestly concentrates his thoughts upon the finding of that life, he practices meditation.

Without intense aspiration, there can be no meditation. Lethargy and indifference are fatal to its practice. The more intense the nature of a man, the more readily will he find meditation, and the more successfully will he practice it. A fiery nature will most rapidly scale the heights of Truth in meditation, when its aspirations have become sufficiently awakened.

Concentration is necessary to worldly success: meditation is necessary to spiritual success. Worldly skill and knowledge are acquired by concentration: spiritual skill and knowledge are acquired by meditation. By concentration a man can scale the highest heights of genius, but he cannot scale the heavenly heights of Truth: to accomplish this, he must meditate.

By concentration a man may acquire the wonderful comprehension and vast power of a Caesar; by meditation he may reach the divine wisdom and perfect peace of a Buddha. The perfection of concentration is power; the perfection of meditation is wisdom.

By concentration, men acquire skill in the doing of the

things of life—in science, art, trade, etc.,—but by meditation, they acquire skill in life itself; in right living, enlightenment, wisdom, etc. Saints, sages, saviors—wise men and divine teachers—are the finished products of holy meditation.

The four stages in concentration are brought into play in meditation; the difference between the two powers being one of direction, and not of nature. Meditation is therefore spiritual concentration; the bringing of the mind to a focus in its search for the divine knowledge, the divine life; the intense dwelling, in thought, on Truth.

Thus a man aspires to know and realize, above all things else, the Truth; he then gives attention to conduct, to life, to self-purification: giving attention to these things, he passes into serious contemplation of the facts, problems, and mystery of life: thus contemplating, he comes to love Truth so fully and intensely as to become wholly absorbed in it, the mind is drawn away from its wanderings in a multitude of desires, and, solving one by one the problems of life, realizes that profound union with Truth which is the state of abstraction; and thus absorbed in Truth, there is that balance and poise of character, that divine action in repose, which is the abiding calm and peace of an emancipated and enlightened mind.

Meditation is more difficult to practice than concentration because it involves a much more severe self-discipline than that which obtains in concentration. A man can practice concentration without purifying his heart and life, whereas the process of purification is inseparable from meditation.

The object of meditation is divine enlightenment, the attainment of Truth, and is therefore interwoven with practical purity and righteousness. Thus while, at first, the time spent in actual meditation is short—perhaps only half an hour in the early morning—the knowledge gained in that half hour of vivid aspiration and concentrated thought is embodied in practice during the whole day.

In meditation, therefore, the entire life of a man is involved; and as he advances in its practice he becomes more and more fitted to perform the duties of life in the circumstances in which he may be placed, for he becomes stronger, holier, calmer, and wiser. The principle of meditation is twofold, namely:

1. Purification of the heart by repetitive thought on pure things.
2. Attainment of divine knowledge by embodying such purity in practical life.

Man is a thought being, and his life and character are determined by the thoughts in which he habitually dwells. By practice, association, and habit, thoughts tend to repeat themselves with greater and greater ease and frequency; and so "fix" the character in a given direction by producing that automatic action which is called "habit."

A powerful and lofty aspiration towards Truth is always accompanied with a keen sense of the sorrow and brevity and mystery of life, and until this condition of mind is reached, meditation is impossible. Merely musing, or whiling away the time in idle dreaming (habits to which the word meditation is frequently applied), are very far removed from meditation, in the lofty spiritual sense which we attach to that condition.

It is easy to mistake reverie for meditation. This is a fatal error which must be avoided by one striving to meditate. The two must not be confounded. Reverie is a loose dreaming into which a man falls; meditation is a strong, purposeful thinking into which a man rises. Reverie is easy and pleasurable; meditation is at first difficult and irksome.

Reverie thrives in indolence and luxury; meditation arises

from strenuousness and discipline. Reverie is first alluring, then sensuous, and then sensual. Meditation is first forbidding, then profitable, and then peaceful. Reverie is dangerous; it undermines self-control. Meditation is protective; it establishes self-control.

There are certain signs by which one can know whether he is engaging in reverie or meditation.

The indications of reverie are:

1.   A desire to avoid exertion.
2.   A desire to experience the pleasures of dreaming.
3.   An increasing distaste for one's worldly duties.
4.   A desire to shirk one's worldly responsibilities.
5.   Fear of consequences.
6.   A wish to get money with as little effort as possible.
7.   Lack of self-control.

The indications of meditation are:

1.   Increase of both physical and mental energy.
2.   A strenuous striving after wisdom.
3.   A decrease of irksomeness in the performance of duty.
4.   A fixed determination to faithfully fulfill all worldly responsibilities.
5.   Freedom from fear.
6.   Indifference to riches.
7.   Possession of self-control.

There are certain times, places, and conditions in and under which it is impossible to meditate, others wherein it is difficult to meditate, and others wherein meditation is rendered more accessible; and these, which should be known and carefully observed, are as follows:

Times, Places, and Conditions in which Meditation is Impossible:

1.   At, or immediately after, meals.
2.   In places of pleasure.
3.   In crowded places.
4.   While walking rapidly.
5.   While lying in bed in the morning.
6.   While smoking.
7.   While lying on a couch or bed for physical or mental relaxation.

Times, Places and Conditions in which Meditation is Difficult:

1.   At night.
2.   In a luxuriously furnished room.
3.   While sitting on a soft, yielding seat.
4.   While wearing gay clothing.
5.   When in company.
6.   When the body is weary.
7.   If the body is given too much food.

Times, Places, and Conditions in which it is Best to Meditate:

1.   Very early in the morning.
2.   Immediately before meals.
3.   In solitude.
4.   In the open air or in a plainly furnished room.
5.   While sitting on a hard seat.
6.   When the body is strong and vigorous.
7.   When the body is modestly and plainly clothed.

It will be seen by the foregoing instructions that ease, luxury, and indulgence (which induce reverie) render meditation difficult, and when strongly pronounced make it impossible; while strenuousness, discipline, and self-denial (which dispel reverie), make meditation comparatively easy. The body, too, should be neither overfed nor starved; neither in rags nor flauntingly clothed. It should not be tired, but should be at its highest point of energy and strength, as the holding of the mind to a concentrated train of subtle and lofty thought requires a high degree of both physical and mental energy.

Aspiration can often best be aroused, and the mind renewed in meditation, by the mental repetition of a lofty precept, a beautiful sentence or a verse of poetry. Indeed, the mind that is ready for meditation will instinctively adopt this practice. Mere mechanical repetition is worthless, and even a hindrance.

The words repeated must be so applicable to one's own condition that they are dwelt upon lovingly and with concentrated devotion. In this way aspiration and concentration harmoniously combine to produce, without undue strain, the state of meditation. All the conditions above stated are of the utmost importance in the early stages of meditation, and should be carefully noted and duly observed by all who are striving to acquire the practice; and those who faithfully follow the instructions, and who strive and persevere, will not fail to gather in, in due season, the harvest of purity, wisdom, bliss, and peace; and will surely eat of the sweet fruits of holy meditation.

26

SERENITY

Calmness of mind is one of the beautiful jewels of wisdom. It is the result of long and patient effort in self-control. Its presence is an indication of ripened experience, and of a more than ordinary knowledge of the laws and operations of thought.

A man becomes calm in the measure that he understands himself as a thought evolved being, for such knowledge necessitates the understanding of others as the result of thought, and as he develops a right understanding, and sees more and more clearly the internal relations of things by the action of cause and effect he ceases to fuss and fume and worry and grieve, and remains poised, steadfast, serene.

The calm man, having learned how to govern himself, knows how to adapt himself to others; and they, in turn, reverence his spiritual strength, and feel that they can learn of him and rely upon him. The more tranquil a man becomes, the greater is his success, his influence, his power for good. Even the ordinary trader will find his business prosperity increase as he develops a greater self-control and equanimity, for people will always prefer to deal with a man whose demeanour is strongly equable.

The strong, calm man is always loved and revered. He is like a shade-giving tree in a thirsty land, or a sheltering rock in a storm. "Who does not love a tranquil heart, a sweet-tempered, balanced life? It does not matter whether it rains or shines, or what changes come to those possessing these blessings, for they are always sweet, serene, and calm. That exquisite poise of character, which we call serenity is the last lesson of culture, the fruitage of the soul. It is precious as wisdom, more to be desired than gold—yea, than even fine gold. How insignificant mere money seeking looks in comparison with a serene life—a life that dwells in the ocean of Truth, beneath the waves, beyond the reach of tempests, in the Eternal Calm!

"How many people we know who sour their lives, who ruin all that is sweet and beautiful by explosive tempers, who destroy their poise of character, and make bad blood! It is a question whether the great majority of people do not ruin their lives and mar their happiness by lack of self-control. How few people we meet in life who are well balanced, who have that exquisite poise which is characteristic of the finished character!

Yes, humanity surges with uncontrolled passion, is tumultuous with ungoverned grief, is blown about by anxiety and doubt only the wise man, only he whose thoughts are controlled and purified, makes the winds and the storms of the soul obey him.

Tempest-tossed souls, wherever ye may be, under whatsoever conditions ye may live, know this: In the ocean of life the isles of Blessedness are smiling, and the sunny shore of your ideal awaits your coming. Keep your hand firmly upon the helm of thought. In the bark of your soul reclines the commanding Master; He does but sleep: wake Him. Self-control is strength; Right Thought is mastery; Calmness is power. Say unto your heart, "Peace, be still!"

27

THE LIGHT THAT NEVER GOES OUT

Amid the multitude of conflicting opinions and theories, and caught in the struggle of existence, whither shall the confused truth-seeker turn to find the path that leads to peace unending? To what refuge shall he fly from the uncertainties and sorrows of change?

Will he find peace in pleasure? Pleasure has its place, and in its place it is good; but as an end, as a refuge, it affords no shelter. He who seeks it as such does but increase the anguish of life; for what is more fleeting than pleasure, and what is more empty than the heart that seeks satisfaction in so ephemeral a thing? There is, therefore, no abiding refuge in pleasure.

Will he find peace in wealth and worldly success?

Wealth and worldly success have their place, but they are fickle and uncertain possessions, and he who seeks them for themselves alone will be burdened with many anxieties and cares. When the storms of adversity sweep over his glittering yet frail habitation, he will find himself helpless and exposed. But even should he maintain such possessions throughout life, what satisfaction will they afford him in the hour of death? There is no abiding refuge in wealth and worldly success.

Will he find peace in health? Health has its place, and it should not be thrown away or despised, but it belongs to the body which is destined for dissolution, and is therefore perishable. Even should health be maintained for a hundred years, the time will come when the physical energies will decline and debility and decay will overtake them. There is no abiding refuge in health.

Will he find refuge in those whom he dearly loves? Those whom he loves have their place in his life. They afford him means of practicing unselfishness, and thereby arriving at Truth. He should cherish them with loving care, and consider their needs before his own. But the time will come when they will be separated from him, and he will be left alone.

There is no abiding refuge in loved ones.

Will he find peace in this Scripture or that? Scripture fills an important place. As a guide it is good, but it cannot be a refuge, for one may know the Scripture by heart, and yet be in sore conflict and unrest. The theories of men are subject to successive changes, and no limit can be set to the variety of textual interpretations. There is no abiding refuge in Scripture.

Will he find rest in this teacher or that? The teacher has his place, and as an instructor he renders good service. But teachers are numerous, and their differences are many. Though one may regard his particular teacher as in possession of the Truth, that teacher will one day be taken from him. There is no abiding refuge in a teacher.

Will he find peace in solitude? Solitude is good and necessary in its place, but he who courts it as a lasting refuge will be like one perishing of thirst in a waterless desert. He will escape men and the turmoil of the city, but he will not escape himself and the unrest of the heart. There is no abiding rest in solitude.

If, then, the seeker can find no refuge in pleasure, in success, in health, in family and friends, in Scripture, in the teacher, or in solitude, whither shall he turn to find that sanctuary which shall afford abiding peace?

Let him take refuge in righteousness. Let him fly to the

sanctuary of a purified heart. Let him enter the pathway of a blameless, stainless life, and walk it meekly and patiently until it brings him to the eternal temple of Truth in his own heart.

He who has taken refuge in Truth, even in the habitation of a wise understanding and a loving and steadfast heart, is the same whether in pleasure or pain; wealth or poverty; success or failure; health or sickness; with friends or without; in solitude or noisy haunts; and he is independent of bibles and teachers, for the spirit of Truth instructs him. He perceives without fear or sorrow the change and decay which are in all things. He has found peace; he has entered the abiding sanctuary; he knows the Light that will never go out.

28

THE TEMPLE OF PROSPERITY

The reader who has followed the course of this book with a view to obtaining information on the details of money making, business transactions, profit and loss in various undertakings, prices, markets, agreements, contracts, and other matters connected with the achievement of prosperity, will have noted an entire absence of any instruction on these matters of detail. The reason for this is fourfold, namely:-

First. Details cannot stand alone, but are powerless to build up anything unless intelligently related to principles.

Second. Details are infinite, and are ceaselessly changing, while principles are few, and are eternal and unchangeable.

Third. Principles are the coherent factors in all details, regulating and harmonizing them, so that to have right principles is to be right in all the subsidiary details.

Fourth. A teacher of truth in any direction must adhere rigidly to principles, and must not allow himself to be drawn away from them into the ever-changing maze of private particulars and personal details, because such particulars and details have only a local right, and are only necessary for certain individuals, while principles are universally right and are necessary for all men.

He who grasps the principles of this book so as to be able to intelligently practice them, will be able to reach the heart of this fourfold reason. The details of a man's affairs are important, but they are his details or the details of his particular branch of industry, and all outside that branch are not concerned with them, but moral principles are the same for all men; they are applicable to all conditions, and govern all particulars.

The man who works from fixed principles does not need to harass himself over the complications of numerous details. He will grasp, as it were, the entire details in one single thought, and will see them through and through, illumined by the light of the principle to which they stand related, and this without friction, and with freedom from anxiety and strain.

Until principles are grasped, details are regarded, and dealt with, as primary matters, and so viewed they lead to innumerable complications and confused issues. In the light of principles, they are seen to be secondary facts, and so seen, all difficulties connected with them are at once overcome and annulled by a reference to principles.

To have the body of prosperity—its material presentation—we must first have the spirit of prosperity, and the spirit of prosperity is the quick spirit of moral virtue. Moral blindness prevails. Men see money, property, pleasure, leisure, etc., and, mistaking them for prosperity, strive to get them for their own enjoyment, but, when obtained, they find no enjoyment in them.

Prosperity is at first a spirit, an attitude of mind, a moral power, a life, which manifests outwardly in the form of plenty, happiness, joy. Just as a man cannot become a genius by writing poems, essay as plays, but must develop and acquire the soul of genius—when the writing will follow as effect to cause-so one cannot become prosperous by hoarding up money, and by gaining property and possessions, but must develop and acquire the soul of virtue, when the material accessories will follow as effect to cause, for the spirit of virtue is the spirit of joy, and it contains within itself all abundance, all satisfaction, all fullness of life.

There is no joy in money, there is no joy in property, there is no joy in material accumulations or in any material things of itself. These things are dead and lifeless. The spirit of joy must be in the man or it is nowhere. He must have within him the capacity for happiness. He must have the wisdom to know how to use these things, and not merely hoard them. He must possess them, and not be possessed by them. They must be dependent upon him, and not he upon them. They must be dependent upon him, and not he upon them. They must follow him, and not be for ever be running after them; and they will inevitably follow him, if he has the moral elements within to which they are related.

Nothing is absent from the Kingdom of heaven; it contains all good, true, and necessary things, and "the Kingdom of God is within you." I know rich people who are supremely happy, because they are generous, magnanimous, pure and joyful; but I also know rich people who are very miserable, and these are they who looked to money and possessions for their happiness, and have not developed the spirit of good and of joy within themselves.

Thus prosperity resolves itself into a moral capacity, and in the wisdom to rightfully use and lawfully enjoy the material things which are inseparable from our earthly life. If one would be free without, let him first be free within, for if he be bound in a spirit by weakness, selfishness, or vice, how can the possession of money liberate him! Will it not rather become, in his hands, a ready instrument by which to further enslave himself?

The moral man is ever blessed, ever happy, and his life, viewed as a whole, is always a success. To these there is no exception, for whatever failures he may have in detail, the finished work of his life will be sound, whole, complete; and through all he will have a quiet conscience, an honorable name, and all manifold blessings which are inseparable from richness of character, and without this moral richness, financial riches will not avail or satisfy.

Let us briefly recapitulate, and again view the Eight Pillars in their strength and splendour.

Energy—Rousing one's self up to strenuous and unremitting exertion in the accomplishment of one's task.

Economy—Concentration of power, the conservation of both capital and character, the latter being mental capital, and therefore of the utmost importance.

Integrity—Unswerving honesty; keeping inviolate all promises, agreements, and contracts, apart from all considerations of loss or gain.

System—Making all details, subservient to order, and thereby relieving the memory and the mind of superfluous work and strain by reducing many to one.

Sympathy—Magnanimity, generosity, gentleness, and tenderness; being open handed, free, and kind.

Sincerity—Being sound and whole, robust and true; and therefore not being one person in public and another in private, and not assuming good actions openly while doing bad actions in secret.

Impartiality—Justice; not striving for self, but weighing both sides, and acting in accordance with equity.

Self-Reliance—Looking to one's self only for strength

and support by standing on principles which are fixed and invincible, and not relying upon outward things which at any moment may be snatched away.

How can any life be other than successful which is built on these Eight Pillars? Their strength is such that no physical or intellectual strength can compare with it; and to have built all the eight perfectly would render a man invincible. It will be found, however, that men are often strong in one or several of these qualities, and weak in others, and it is this weak element that invites failure. It is foolish, for instance, to attribute a man's failure in business to his honest. Honesty can't produce failure. The cause of failure must be looked for in some other direction—in the lack, and not the possession, of some good necessary quality. Moreover, such attribution of failure to honesty is a slur on the integrity of commerce; and a false indictment of those men, numerous enough, who are honourably engaged in trade. A man may be strong in Energy, Economy, and System, but comparatively weak in the other five. Such a man will just fail of complete success by lacking one of the four corner pillars, namely, Integrity. His temple will give way at that weak corner, for the first four Pillars must be well built before the Temple of Prosperity can stand secure.

He who so abides by these four principles will achieve a full measure of success in his own particular work, whatever it may be; his Temple of Prosperity will be well built and well supported, and it will stand secure. The perfect practice of these four principles is within the scope of all men who are willing to study them with that object in view, for they are so simple and plain that a child could grasp their meaning, and their perfection in conduct does not call for an unusual degree of self sacrifice, though it demands some self denial and personal discipline without which there can be no success in this world of action. The second four pillars, however, are principles of a more profound nature, are more difficult to understand and practice, and call from the highest degree of self sacrifice and self effacement. Few, at present, can reach that detachment from the personal element which their perfect practice demands, but the few who accomplish this in any marked degree will vastly enlarge their powers and enrich their life, and will adorn their Temple of Prosperity with a singular and attractive beauty which will gladden and elevate all beholders long after they have passed away.

But those who are beginning to build their Temple of Prosperity in accordance with the teaching of this book, must bear in mind that a building requires time to erect, and it must be patiently raised up, brick upon brick and stone upon stone, and the Pillars must be firmly fixed and cemented, and labour and care will be needed to make the whole complete. And the building of this inner mental Temple is none the less real and substantial because invisible and noiseless, for in the raising up of his, as of Solomon's Temple which was "seven years in building"—it can be said, "there was neither hammer nor axe nor any tool of iron heard in the house, while it was in the building".

Even so, oh reader construct thy character, raise up the house of thy life, build up thy Temple of Prosperity. Be not as the foolish who rise and fall upon the uncertain flux of selfish desires: but be at peace in thy labour, crown thy career with completeness, and so be numbered among the wise who, without uncertainty, build upon a fixed and secure foundation— even upon the Principles of Truth which endure for ever.

29

KNOWLEDGE AND VICTORY

Faith is the beginning of the Triumphant Life, but knowledge is its consummation. Faith reveals the way, but knowledge is the goal. Faith suffers many afflictions; knowledge has transcended affliction. Faith endures; knowledge loves. Faith walks in darkness, but believes; knowledge acts in light, and knows. Faith inspires to effort; knowledge crowns effort with success. "Faith is the substance of things hoped for"; knowledge is the substance of those things possessed. Faith is the helpful staff of the pilgrim; knowledge is the City of Refuge at the journey's end. Without faith there will be no knowledge, but when knowledge is acquired, the work of faith is finished.

The Life Triumphant is a life of knowledge; and by knowledge is meant, not booklearning, but life-learning; not superficial facts committed to memory, but the deep facts and truths of life, grasped and comprehended. Apart from this knowledge there is no victory for man, no rest for his weary feet, no refuge for His aching heart.

There is no salvation for the foolish except by becoming wise. There is no salvation for the sinful except by becoming pure. There is no liberation for man from the turmoil and troubles of life but through divine knowledge reached by the pathway of a pure and blameless life. Nowhere is there permanent peace except in an enlightened condition of mind; and a pure life and an enlightened mind are identical.

But there is salvation for the foolish because wisdom can

be acquired. There is salvation for the sinful because purity can be embraced. There is liberation for all men from the troubles and turmoil of life because whosoever wills to do so—whether rich or poor, learned or unlearned—can enter the lowly way of blamelessness which leads to perfect knowledge. And because of this—that there is deliverance for the captives and victory for the defeated—there is rejoicing in the High Places, and the universe is glad.

The man of knowledge, being victorious over himself, is victorious over sin, over evil, over all the disharmonies of life. Out of the old mind marred by sin and sorrow, he has framed a new mind glorified by purity and peace. He has died out of the old world of evil, and is reborn in a new world where love and faultless law prevail, where evil is not, and he has become deathless in immortal Good.

Anxiety and fear, grief and lamentation, disappointment and regret, wretchedness and remorse—these things have no part in the world of the wise. They are the shadowy inhabitants of the world of self, and cannot five, nay, they are seen to have no substantiality—in the light of wisdom. The dark things of life are the dark conditions of a mind not yet illuminated by the light of wisdom. They follow self as the shadow of substance. Where selfish desires go, there they follow; where sin is, there they are. There is no rest in self; there is no light in self. And where the flames of turbulent passions and fires of consuming desires are rife, the cool airs of wisdom and peace are not felt.

Safety and assurance, happiness and repose, satisfaction and contentment, joy and peace—these are the abiding possessions of the wise, earned by right of selfconquest, the results of righteousness, the wages of a blameless life.

The substance of a right life is enlightenment (knowledge), and the spirit of knowledge is peace. To be victorious over self in all the issues of life is to know life as it is in reality, and not as it appears in the nightmare of self. It is to be in peace in all passages, and not to be stricken with trouble and grief in the common happenings of life.

As the ripe scholar is no more troubled by incorrect work and lessons imperfectly done, and the painful reproof and punishment formerly inflicted by his teachers are left behind forever, so the perfected scholar in virtue, the wise man and woman, the enlightened doer of righteousness, is no more troubled with wrongdoing and folly (which are merely the imperfectly accomplished lessons of life), and the scourging of sorrow and remorse have passed away forever.

The skilled scholar has no more doubt or fear concerning his ability. He has overcome and dispersed the ignorance of his intellect. He has attained to learning, and he knows that he has attained. And he so knows because, having undergone innumerable tests in the forms of lessons and examinations, he has at last proved his skill by passing successfully through the severest tests of scholarship. And now he no longer fears, but rejoices when severe tests are applied to prove his ability. He is capable, confident, and glad.

Even so the skilled doer of righteousness is no more troubled with doubt and fear concerning his destiny. He has overcome and dispersed the ignorance of his heart. He has attained to wisdom, and he knows that he has attained. And he so knows because where he formerly failed and fell when tested by the wrong conduct of others, he now maintains his patience and calmness under the severest tests of accusation and reproof.

Herein is the glory and victory of divine knowledge, that understanding the nature of deeds, both good and bad, the enlightened doer of good deeds no longer suffers through the bad deeds of others. Their actions towards him can never cause him pain and sorrow, nor rob him of his peace. Having taken refuge in good, evil can no more reach nor harm him. He returns good for evil, and overcomes the weakness of evil by the power of good.

The man who is involved in bad deeds imagines that the bad deeds of others are powerful to do him injury and are filled with grievous harm against him. He is stung with pain and overwhelmed with sorrow, not for his own bad deeds (for these he does not see) but for the wrong deeds of others. Involved in ignorance, he has no spiritual strength, no refuge, and no abiding peace.

The man victorious over self is the true seer. He is not the seer of spirits or supernatural phenomena, for such seeing is narrow and illusory. He is the seer of life as it is, both in its particular aspects and in its divine principles; the seer of the spiritual universe of cosmic law, cosmic love, and cosmic liberty.

The man of knowledge and victory, who has shaken off the painful dreams of self, has awakened with a new vision which beholds a new and glorified universe, He is the seer of the Eternal, and is blessed with perfect love and endless peace. He is lifted far above all sordid desires, narrow aims, and selfish love and hate; and being so lifted up he perceives the lawful course of things, and does not grieve when overtaken by the inevitable. He is above the world of sorrow, not because he has become cold and cruel, but because he abides in a love where no thought of self can enter, and where the well-being of others is all-in-all. He is sorrowless because he is selfless. He is serene because he knows that whatever he receives, it is good, and whatever is taken from him, that also is good. He has transmuted sorrow into love, and is filled with infinite tenderness and abounding compassion. His power is not violent, ambitious, worldly, but pure, peaceful, heavenly, and he is possessed of a hidden strength which knows how to stand and when to bend for the good of others and the world.

He is a Teacher, though he speaks but little. He is a Master, yet he has no desire to rule others. He is a Conqueror, but makes no attempt to subdue his fellow men. He has become a conscious instrument for the outworking of cosmic law, and is an intelligent, enlightened power directing the evolution of the Race.

At this, the beginning of a new epoch, let the Good News again go forth throughout the world that there is purity for the sinful, comfort for the afflicted, healing for the broken-hearted, and triumph for the defeated. In your heart, O man! O woman! stained as it is with sin, and torn with conflicting desires, there is a place of power, a citadel of strength. You are the dwelling-place of the Supreme Good, and the Scepter of Victory awaits you: deep in your consciousness is the High Seat of Empire. Arise, O stricken one! Ascend your rightly throne!

30

MAN THE MASTER

By the mastery of self, a distinct form of consciousness is evolved which some would call divine. It is distinguished from that ordinary human consciousness, which craves personal advantages and gratifications on the one hand, and is involved in remorse and sorrow on the other. This divine consciousness concerns itself with humanity and the universe, with eternal verities, with righteousness, wisdom, and truth, and not with pleasures, protection, and preservation of the personality. Not that personal pleasure is destroyed, but that it is no longer craved and sought, it no longer takes a foremost place. It is purified, and it is received as the effect of right thought and action, and is no longer an end in itself.

In divine consciousness there is neither sin nor sorrow. Even the sense of sin has passed away, and the true order and purpose of life being revealed, no cause is found for lamentation. Jesus called this state of consciousness "The Kingdom of Heaven"; Buddha named it "Nirvana"; Lao-Tze's term for it was "Tao"; Emerson refers to it as "The Over-Soul"; and Dr. Bucke calls it "Cosmic Consciousness" in his valuable work bearing that title.

The ordinary human consciousness is self-consciousness. Self, the personality, is placed before everything else. There are ceaseless anxieties and fears concerning the self. Its possible loss is thought to be the most grievous calamity, and its eternal preservation the most important thing in the universe.

In divine consciousness all this has passed away. Self has disappeared. Therefore, there can be no more fears and anxieties concerning the self, and things are considered and known as they are, and not as they afford pleasure or cause pain to self, not as self wishes them to be for its own temporal or eternal happiness.

The self-conscious man is subject to desire; the divinely conscious man is master of desire. The former considers what is pleasant or unpleasant; the latter acts from the righteous law without reference to pleasure or pain.

The race is passing through self-consciousness to divine consciousness; through the slavery of self, with its sense of sin and shame, to the freedom of Truth, with its sense of purity and power. The Great Teachers and Saviors of the race have already attained. In former existences they have already passed through all forms of selfconsciousness, and now, having subjugated self, have become divinely conscious.

They have reached the summit of evolution on this earth, and have no further need to be reborn in the self-conscious form. They are Masters of Life. Having conquered self, they have acquired the Supreme Knowledge. Some of them are worshiped as God because they manifest a wisdom and a consciousness which is quite distinct from the normal self-consciousness of humanity, and which is therefore regarded with, and surrounded by, incomprehensible mystery. Yet, in this divine consciousness there is no mystery, but, on the contrary, a transparent simplicity which becomes apparent when the confusions of self are dispersed.

The abiding gentleness, the sublime wisdom, the perfect calm of the Great Teachers—qualities which appear supernatural when viewed from the selfconsciousness state— are seen to be simple and natural when the first glimmering of divine consciousness dawns in the mind. And such divine consciousness does not appear until a high degree of morality is attained by self-conscious man.

Man becomes divinely conscious, divinely wise, divinely gentle and strong in the measure that he subdues and dominates within, those passions by which humanity is subdued and dominated. The divine master is one who has attained mastery over self. The abiding nobility, beneficent characteristics, and unobtrusive virtue which mark off the spiritually enlightened man from others, are the fruits of self-conquest, the logical outcome of a long struggle to master and comprehend those mental forces which the self-conscious man blindly obeys without understanding.

Self-conscious man is a slave to self. Obeying self-centered inclinations, he is in submission to his passions, and to the sorrows and pains which allegiance to those passions inflict upon him. He is conscious of sin and sorrow, but sees no way out of these conditions. And so he invents theologies which he substitutes for effort, and which, while affording him fitful comfort through uncertain hope, leave him the easy victim of sin, and the willing prey of sorrow.

Divinely conscious man is the master of self. He obeys Truth and not self. He curbs and directs his inclinations and is conscious of a growing power over sin and sorrow. He sees that there is a way out of these conditions by the path of self-mastery. He needs no theologies to aid him, but exerts himself in right-doing, and is gladdened by a sense of victory and increasing purity and power. When his mastery is complete, he has no inclinations but those which accord with Truth. He has then become the conqueror of sin, and is no longer subject to sorrow.

Enlightened, wise, and evermore peaceful and happy is he who has subjected, overcome, and cast out the turbulent self that reigned within. The tempests of sorrow do not chill him. The cares and troubles which beset man pass him by, and no evil thing overtakes him. Secure in divine virtue, no enemy can overthrow him; no foe can do harm. Kind and peaceful, no person, power, nor place can rob him of repose.

There is no enemy but self, no darkness but ignorance, no suffering but that which springs from the insubordinate elements of one's own nature.

No man is truly wise who is involved in likes and dislikes, wishes and regrets, desires and disappointments, sins and sorrow. All these conditions belong to the selfconscious state, and are indications of folly, weakness, and subjection.

He is truly wise who, in the midst of worldly duties, is always calm, always gentle, always patient. He accepts things as they are, and does not wish nor grieve, desire nor regret. These things belong to the divinely conscious state, the dominion of Truth, and are indications of enlightenment, strength, and mastery.

He who does not desire riches, fame, or pleasures; who enjoys what he has, yet does not lament when it is taken from him, he is indeed wise.

He who desires riches, fame, and pleasure; who is discontented with what he has, yet laments when it is taken from him, he is indeed foolish.

Man is fitted for conquest, but the conquest of territory will not avail; he must resort to the conquest of self. The conquest of territory renders man a temporal ruler, but the conquest of self makes him an eternal conqueror.

Man is destined for mastery; not the mastery of his fellow men by force, but the mastery of his own nature by self-control. The mastery of his fellow men by force is the crown of egotism, but the mastery of self by self-control is the crown of humility.

He is man the master who has shaken off the service of self for the service of Truth, who has established himself in the Eternal Verities. He is crowned, not only with perfect manhood, but with divine wisdom. He has overcome the disturbances of the mind and the shocks of life. He is superior to all circumstances. He is the calm spectator, but no longer the helpless tool, of events. No more a sinning, weeping, repenting mortal, he is pure, rejoicing, upright immortal. He perceives the course of things with a glad and peaceful heart; a divine conqueror, master of life and death.

Made in the USA
Monee, IL
07 July 2026